LIVE
While You're
ALIVE

LIVE
While You're
ALIVE

Shiv Khera

B L O O M S B U R Y
NEW DELHI • LONDON • OXFORD • NEW YORK • SYDNEY

BLOOMSBURY INDIA
Bloomsbury Publishing India Pvt. Ltd
Second Floor, LSC Building No. 4, DDA Complex,
Pocket C – 6 & 7, Vasant Kunj,
New Delhi 110070

BLOOMSBURY, BLOOMSBURY INDIA and the Diana logo are
trademarks of Bloomsbury Publishing Plc

First published in India 2025
This edition published 2025

ISBN: PB: 978-93-90513-74-1; eBook: 978-93-90513-76-5
2 4 6 8 10 9 7 5 3 1

Printed and bound in India by Thomson Press India Ltd

To find out more about our authors and books, visit
www.bloomsbury.com and sign up for our newsletters

MR. SHIV KHERA is an author, educator, business consultant and a much sought-after speaker.

He inspires and encourages individuals to realize their true potential. He has taken his dynamic personal messages to opposite sides of the globe, from the U.S. to Singapore. His 40 years of research and understanding has put millions on the path of growth and fulfillment.

Over **13 million copies** of his books have been sold globally including his international bestseller *You Can Win* in 21 languages.

His clients include **Lufthansa, HP, DHL, HSBC, Canon, Nestlé, Philips, Mercedes, Johnson & Johnson, MetLife** and many more.

Tens of thousands have benefited from his **dynamic workshops internationally** in over 20 countries and **millions** have heard him as a **keynote speaker**. He has appeared on numerous radio and television shows.

Mr. Khera is the brand ambassador of Round Table Foundation. He has been honored by The Lions International and Rotary International.

His Trademark is
**'Winners don't do different things,
They do things differently.'**

To
My mother, for being my North Star
My wife, who is my soulmate
My children and grandchildren,
who are my most precious relationships
And God, for His choicest blessings

Contents

Preface

Why did I choose the title *Live While You're Alive*? Sadly, most people live with a false notion that you only live once. This book is a life manual that helps you to live in an effective, meaningful and happy way. It clarifies the difference between little and crucial and petty and trivial.

Circumstances do not make a man; they only reveal him to himself. How come under the same set of circumstances, some people break records while others break themselves? All of us can handle stress, but what we cannot handle is chronic stress. Stress, if handled properly, energizes people; if not, it drains them. It can bring sickness, lead to ill health, shorten life, ruin relationships and make life miserable. However, when stress is managed well, it can be a cause of success.

We cannot have a positive life with a negative mindset. Choosing calmness over chaos is a conscious response. We must live by the philosophy of prepare and prevent rather than repair and repent. In life, we cannot choose the cards that are dealt to us, but we can always choose how we play the game.

Although the insights given in this book are timeless, their importance is greater now than ever before. It provides you with the tools to handle stress effectively, resulting in good health, prosperity, happiness and meaningful relationships.

Acknowledgments

Any accomplishment requires the effort of many people, and this book is no different. I thank my daughters and especially my wife, whose patience and support was instrumental in accomplishing this task. I thank my staff, whose diligent efforts made this publication possible.

Many examples, stories, anecdotes are the result of a collection from various sources, such as newspapers, magazines, other speakers and participants at seminars, over the past twenty-five years. Unfortunately, sources were not always noted or available; hence, it became impractical to provide an accurate acknowledgment. Regardless of the source, I wish to express my gratitude to those who may have contributed to this work, even though anonymously.

Every effort has been made to give credit where it is due for the material contained herein. If inadvertently we have missed giving credit, future editions will give due credit to those that are brought to the author's attention.

There is a saying that
we only live once.
This is not true.
We only die once.
We live every day
provided we know
how to live.

1

Respond, Don't React

John was going to the office when a car from behind hit his car's bumper. He got out of his car furious and ready to fight, and he shouted: 'You ruined my car, you ruined my day.' Right from the time he entered his office, he spread his negativity and anger all around. The atmosphere in the office got stressful and negative, thus demoralizing everyone. None of the people could concentrate on their work. This led to more mistakes, and the quality of output dropped, which created further stress. It became a vicious circle. It did not end there.

John's secretary was upset all day long. She took her anger home and shouted at her son. The son, who was looking forward to playing with his mother, kicked his little pup in anger. The pup sat quietly in a corner, feeling sad.

Look at the ripple effect. Negativity is contagious. But positivity can be contagious too.

Let's look at another situation.

Steve was on his way to the office. Near the bridge, his car turned turtle. Steve wriggled out of the window unhurt. The car was a total loss. When Steve came out of the window, he said to himself: 'What a lucky day! The good Lord must have been riding with me. I came out unscathed.' He reached his office in a great mood and said to everybody, 'Man, what a lucky day,' and he spread that joy everywhere. He converted his brush with death into an occasion of joy and celebration and that brought positivity to the entire environment. It motivated everyone to focus and do a great job. The quality and quantity of output went up. Steve and everyone around him had a great day. It became a cycle of positive energy and happiness.

In the above examples, both people met with mishaps which were possibly beyond their control and the trigger was a car accident. One was minor; the other was major. But John blew it out of proportion, and Steve was grateful to be lucky. The question is, what caused the difference in their behaviors? Was it the accident or was it their response to the accident? It was their response to their respective situations. Steve was responding. John was reacting.

Responding is positive. Reacting is negative.

Respond, Don't React. Reacting to situations is negative, whereas responding is positive. While facing a crisis, we should respond, not react. What is the difference? When the doctor says you are reacting to a medicine, it is a danger sign. That means something negative is happening.

When you tell your doctor, 'I am feeling better with the treatment,' the doctor says, 'Great, you are responding well to the treatment.' But if you say, 'I have three side effects,' the doctor will say, 'Let me change the treatment because the medicine has reacted.'

In life, it is not our position but our disposition that determines success. And what is disposition? Disposition is our attitude. To some people shopping is relaxing; to others it's a nightmare. Does everyone relax in the same manner? The answer is no.

Under the same set of circumstances, how come some people break records while others break themselves?

Learn to respond, not react. Learn to be proactive. Proactive people see an opportunity in every obstacle. They see every stone as a stepping stone, not a stumbling block. When something goes wrong in their life, they ask themselves two questions:

(a) What lesson have I learned?

(b) What could have been worse?

They learn from the experience, stand up, dust themselves and restart with a positive attitude. To them every obstacle is a learning opportunity. They are in charge and in control of their lives. They act, not react.

Let's now move on to an activity. At the end of each chapter of this book I will ask you a set of questions or list some activities that will prompt you to look inward and hopefully drive you to make changes in your life.

Life is 10 percent what happens to you and 90 percent how you respond to it.

ACTIVITY

1. Identify one major take-home from this chapter.

   _____

   _____

   _____

2. Do you habitually respond proactively in a positive manner like Steve or do you react negatively like John?

   _____

   _____

   _____

3. What trait/behavior would you like to change in yourself to respond in a positive manner?

   _____

   _____

   _____

4. I commit to responding in a positive manner to every situation in life.

You cannot have a positive life with a negative mindset.

2

Management/ Mismanagement

A man went to his spiritual master and said, 'I'm fed up with my work; my boss is nasty. I'm overworked, underpaid and exhausted. Show me a direction and give me your blessings.' The teacher asked, 'If you're so fed up, do you want me to bless you that you be fired? Would that make you happy?' The man said, 'No, master, that will create a bigger problem.' The teacher replied, 'You have a job, you have a problem; you don't have a job, you have a bigger problem. Don't you see that the problem is not with the job, it is your mismanagement?'

Our stress and tension have nothing to do with our job. It is our ability or inability to manage our mind, finances, health and relationships that causes stress and tension. Proper management of these results in positive outcomes; mismanagement leads to negative results.

- Managing finances brings profit. Mismanagement of finances causes loss.
- Managing health brings profit. Mismanagement of health causes loss.
- Managing relationships brings profit. Mismanagement of relationships causes loss.

If people are poor, they suffer from deprivation. If they are rich, they suffer from paying too much in taxes. If they are uneducated, they suffer from ignorance. If they are educated, they suffer from conceit. If they are single, they suffer from loneliness. If they are married, they suffer from friction. The problem is not with the situation, it is with their mismanagement.

Is your mind being directed or being misdirected by you?

- If you're alone and feeling lonely, that is mismanagement.
- If you're in the company of others and yet miserable and lonely, that is mismanagement.
- If you're alone and at peace with yourself, it means you are enjoying solitude. That is good management.

Stress does not discriminate – it impacts equally the rich and the poor, the young and the old, the celebrated and the unknown.

- Loss of productivity due to depression and anxiety cost the global economy approximately $1 trillion.[1]
- Stress-caused absenteeism among workers in the workplace is an estimated 1 million globally.[2]
- It is estimated that job stress results in over $300 billion in losses for the U.S. industry, primarily due to absenteeism, reduced productivity, and workplace accidents.[3]
- 83 percent of U.S. workers say they suffer from daily work-related stress.[4]

Mismanagement can turn a great idea into a disaster.

ACTIVITY

1. Identify one major take-home from this chapter.

   _____

   _____

   _____

2. Identify one area of your life where you can avoid mismanagement.

   _____

   _____

   _____

3. I commit to changing the following behavior:

   _____

   _____

   _____

We cannot choose
the cards that are
dealt to us; we can
only choose how to
play the hand.

3

Attitude Is Everything

A young couple went on a holiday to Mauritius. They stayed at a luxurious five-star hotel by the seaside. The ambience and the service were par excellence. As they entered their room, the husband saw that the room wasn't facing the sea. This was the only room available as the hotel was totally sold out. He threw a fit and created a ruckus. The wife tried to appeal to logic and pacify him. She said it was a minor thing and didn't really matter. It was inconsequential to the larger picture of being together.

But the husband didn't understand at all. He confronted the receptionist, who in turn called the general manager. The general manager extended all the courtesy and apologized for something that was beyond his control. He told him that there was no specific request made for a sea-view room at the time of booking. Had they done that, the hotel would have ensured that they got it. His wife again tried to soothe him but to no avail. She tried to explain that the hotel couldn't do anything now. She wanted him to let go of his rigidity so they could enjoy their vacation. She told him, 'Honey, our being together is more important than a sea-view room.' Sea-view was only incidental. He, however, was hell-bent on a sea-view room and just would not see reason. More arguments ensued. He told his *wife that instead of being supportive of him and seeing things from his perspective, she was justifying on behalf of the hotel. This created an insurmountable rift between them throughout the vacation. They didn't talk to each other, didn't eat at the same table and didn't go out sightseeing together. What was meant to be a dream vacation turned into a nightmare. The unpleasant vacation got over five days later. But it didn't end there. The negative memories lingered on in the subconscious. The scar was permanent.*

Such scars leave a lasting impact and eventually result in greater damage. The following questions arise:

- Who created this stress?
- Was it called for?
- Was it avoidable?

It was totally avoidable! The husband could have overlooked the trivial matter – sea-view room – and concentrated on the bigger picture of spending quality time together, which was what the vacation was all about anyway.

The above example may be a slight exaggeration. But such things do happen.

Sometimes therapists advise a change of environment or location or recommend going on a holiday as a remedy to overcome stress. But the way I see it, people with a negative attitude, such as the man in the story above, create stress wherever they go.

Often, when people complain that they are troubled, they are advised a change of scene, going to the movies, taking a vacation, etc. But people carry their troubles to the movie theaters and to the vacation spots. Changing the backdrop doesn't help – running away from problems doesn't help the situation. Stress remains intact. No matter what you do or where you go, stress follows.

Change of environment, location and place is not a remedy for stress.

Change of attitude is the remedy for stress.

ACTIVITY

1. Identify one major take-home from this chapter.

   _____

   _____

   _____

2. Identify an incident where your negative attitude led to stress in your life.

   _____

   _____

   _____

3. I commit to changing the following behavior:

   _____

   _____

   _____

All of us can handle stress, but what we cannot handle is chronic stress.

4

What Is Stress?

Stress is our response to any event or change. **We experience stress whether we like it or not. It is unavoidable.** Confronted by change, we either handle things well or buckle under pressure. Stress can be a source of either 'strength' or 'strain'. It is mental, physical or emotional pressure. Stress that causes strain comes from our inability to handle a particular situation and the resultant helplessness. It is the outcome of a feeling of not being in charge or of things being out of our control.

Let's take the example of a guitar to see how stress can be experienced as strength or strain. The guitar strings must have the right kind of tension for a skillful player to produce music. The instrument cannot be played if the strings are too loose; if the strings are too tight, they will break. But if the guitar is tuned at the optimal point, that is, just right, it will give the desired outcome, which is beautiful music. We need to learn to tune ourselves to just the right level.

Physical stress can be positive or negative. Positive stress prepares you to face the challenge and perform well, whereas negative stress is unsettling.

Mental stress is related to our attitude, the way we think and the way we act or react. It pertains to being optimistic or pessimistic. A positive mind is wise and balanced. A negative mind is troubled and pessimistic.

Emotional stress makes us insecure and pulls us down. Positive impacts are uplifting and energizing and make us feel secure.

Who is responsible for our stress? **Stress needs to be handled by each person individually. It cannot be delegated. It is our attitude and the way we look at any situation that determines our response to stress.**

Chronic Stress

There is the oft-quoted story about the weight of a glass of water that demonstrates the impact of stress on our lives.

A psychologist took a glass of water and asked his audience, 'How heavy do you think this glass is?' and the audience said, 'Maybe a pound or two.' He said, 'The weight of the glass is insignificant, and if I hold it as it is for a minute or two, it is still no big deal. But if I hold it for an hour, I might start feeling discomfort. If I hold it for two hours, my arm would start aching and become stiff. If I hold it any longer than two hours, I might start developing cramps and my arm would go numb, forcing me to drop the glass. Keep in mind that the weight of the glass does not change. But the longer I hold it, the heavier it feels.'

In life stress and worries are very much like this glass of water. In the short run, we can easily handle a small challenge, but if we hold it too long, it becomes painful and eventually we become incapacitated.

What is the moral of the story? All of us can handle stress for short durations, but when stress becomes constant that's the time we break down.

What Is Chronic Stress?

Chronic stress is 'continued stress'. It is an emotional pressure suffered over a prolonged period. **Prolonged stress can wear us out prematurely and lead to burnout or a breakdown.** Over time, chronic stress can accumulate and lead to physical and mental exhaustion, accelerating the aging process.

We cannot handle chronic stress because:

- **It is constant and ongoing.**
- **It keeps draining us drop by drop and is torturous.**

Our biggest challenge is not the stress itself but how we handle it. Not all stress is bad; only when stress becomes a way of life does it start taking a toll on us, and then it becomes chronic stress. In other words, it becomes fatigue, that is, you constantly feel tired mentally and physically. **Chronic stress eats into us bit by bit till it leads to complete destruction.**

Stress Makes Us Perform

Stress is the price we pay to be a racehorse. If you have been to a racecourse and seen thoroughbreds being escorted to their cabin right before the race, you would have noticed that the horse does not walk in a cool and relaxed manner. It will be edgy and agitated because it is under heavy stress. The moment the bell rings and the door opens, it shoots out like a bullet. That is a racehorse. It is the stress that makes it perform. But if we take a jackass to the racecourse, it will walk around casually, totally ignorant about what the place stands for, and exhibit no symptoms of stress. But then, it is a jackass and will remain a jackass. It will never be a thoroughbred nor ever perform like one. **Stress is the price we pay to be a thoroughbred.**

Something similar happens to different performers:

- **An athlete** just before a competition. Is he under stress? The answer is yes. It is the stress that makes him perform. If he had no stress, he would not perform to his peak potential.
- **A public speaker.** It is the same for public speaking: when a speaker gets on to the stage, he has butterflies in his stomach, but a good public speaker makes the butterflies fly in formation. He controls his stress. That is what makes him speak well.

Stress causes three kinds of responses in us: **fight, flight or freeze**. It could be explained as 'natural'. When we see a wild bear in the forest, we respond physically, mentally, and emotionally. Our body releases hormones that trigger our response to fight, to take flight or to freeze.

It is important to note that our responses to stress are physical, mental and emotional. In other words, stress is our response to any event or change.

- **Fight:** Your physical and mental mechanisms get prepared to take on the challenge. Your reflexes respond to support your action.
- **Flight:** When you have no hope and you want to flee. The survival instinct takes over, and you want to escape the terrifying situation.

- **Freeze:** The response to a traumatic situation where you are paralyzed like a deer facing the headlights. It is a state of surrender, a state of hopelessness and helplessness.

Stress happens whether we like it or not. It is unavoidable.

ACTIVITY

1. Identify one major take-home from this chapter.

   _____

   _____

   _____

2. Identify one area in your life where you are experiencing chronic stress.

   _____

   _____

   _____

3. How do you plan to overcome it?

   _____

   _____

   _____

5

The Serenity Prayer

About forty-five years ago, I sat through a program by Dr. Norman Vincent Peale as a student. As he came in, he gave a very confident look to the entire audience and said, 'You all look very comfortable and peaceful. It seems nobody has any problems. Does anyone have a problem?' Well, who doesn't – everybody raised their hands. He then asked how many people would like to get rid of their problems. Again, everybody raised their hands. He said, 'On my way here to this congregation, I came across a place where I saw some people lying down, all stretched out, totally relaxed, and they had no problem whatsoever. How many people would like to know where that place is?' Everybody raised their hands. He said, 'Two blocks away from here there is a cemetery. There are people lying there, all stretched out, comfortable, totally relaxed. They have no problems whatsoever. How many people would like to get rid of their problems?' Nobody raised their hand. In fact, some people put their hands into their pockets. Then Dr. Peale said, 'Problems are a sign of life, and so long as we are alive we shall have problems. The day we do not have problems we will be dead. We cannot solve all our problems, but we can handle them.' That day, he shared with us a prayer called the Serenity Prayer written by the theologian Dr. Reinhold Niebuhr.

God grant me the serenity to accept the things that I cannot change, the courage to change the things I can, and the wisdom to know the difference.

If one analyzes this prayer, the way I see it, it is the gist of life.

It says, 'God grant me the serenity to accept the things that I cannot change.' The question is, is everything within our control in life? The answer is no. There are some things beyond our control. For example, I didn't choose my parents. I didn't decide where I was going to be born. If I am 5'6", I cannot be 6'10". If I am brown-skinned, there is nothing I can do about that. Granted, sometimes people are born with physical and mental challenges. What wrong did they do? Who knows. Granted, sometimes bad things happen to good people for no fault of theirs. What wrong did they do? Who knows. There are some things in life that we just cannot change. We need to accept them as they are. Often we keep fighting the things that we cannot change, and we bring stress into our lives. We become paralyzed and unproductive.

The prayer goes on to say that if I can change things, then please give me the courage to do it.

Lastly, I need the wisdom to know the difference. Because the ability to discern between what one can change and cannot change is key to managing stress. The fact is that life is full of choices and life is full of compromises. Here are a few examples.

How is life full of choices?

- If I ill-treat you, I have chosen to be ill-treated. Haven't I?
- If I treat you with discourtesy, I have chosen to be treated with discourtesy. Haven't I?
- If I eat too much every day, I have chosen to be obese. Haven't I?
- If I light up a cigarette, I have chosen to invite cancer. Haven't I?
- If I exercise every day, I have chosen to invite good health. Haven't I?
- If I drink and drive, I have chosen to invite an accident. Haven't I?
- If I tell lies, I have chosen to lose my credibility. Haven't I?
- If I tell the truth, I have chosen to be trustworthy. Haven't I?[5]

We are all free to the point of choice, but after we make our choices, the choice controls the chooser, and we have no more choice.

All through life, every day, we make hundreds of choices. The kind of work we do, the kind of friends we have, the place we live in, the food we eat, the clothes we wear, the time we go to bed, whether we exercise or not. They are all choices. When our values are clear, decision-making on what choices to make becomes a lot easier even though some are not easy decisions.

In every choice we make and every decision we take, there is a tradeoff and a payoff.

Choices

Problems do affect our life. Everything in life will not go our way. The inability to handle problems effectively can lead to undesirable consequences. The power to make positive choices is really the key to handling stress.

However, making positive choices is not enough. It requires decisive action. Choices without action can be more stressful.

How is life full of compromises?

We cannot choose the cards that are dealt to us, but we can always choose how we play the game. We cannot choose the direction of the wind, but we can always choose how we set the sail. Granted, sometimes nature gives us a lemon. The choice is ours, to cry or to make lemonade!

Many times I am asked, 'Mr. Khera, people who are successful, don't they make mistakes? And the people who fail, don't they do positive things in life?' And my answer is that making a mistake once in a while does not bring failure, repeating the same mistake again and again is what brings failure. Similarly, doing something positive once in a while does not bring success, repeating the positive behavior again and again is what brings success.

What is success?

A series of positive decisions in life is called success and a series of negative decisions is called failure.

ACTIVITY

1. Identify one major take-home from this chapter.

    _____

    _____

    _____

2. Identify three areas in your life where you can make positive choices.

    _____

    _____

    _____

3. Identify three areas where you can change your behavior to bring about positive outcomes.

    _____

    _____

    _____

4. How would you benefit by making the above changes?

    _____

    _____

    _____

6

Get Into the Habit of Finishing What You Start

It is not what you start that matters but what you finish. It is not how much we eat that matters but how much we digest. Some people are good starters but poor finishers. They start with great enthusiasm, but somewhere they lose focus and interest with the result that their projects get abandoned or remain incomplete; for example, people commonly make New Year's resolutions for many things including to get on an exercise regime, and they join a health club in January, but it is also not unusual to see that most health club memberships expire within the first few months.

Similarly, people enroll in classes to learn music, martial arts or other hobbies and skills but only to see the enthusiasm die in a couple of months or even a few weeks.

Why do people quit?

1. They are **noncommittal**. Problems are a part of life; no matter what we do or where we are, they are bound to happen. People who are noncommittal

quit the moment they come across a problem.
When committed people run into a problem or fail
to meet a benchmark, they have a choice to either
increase the effort and achieve the goal or lower the
benchmark and quit. Winners increase the effort
and losers quit.

2. **Unrealistic expectations.** Many times we have
    unrealistic expectations of ourselves. We want to
    become proficient overnight, but sadly, it never
    happens. Hence we get disheartened and we
    quit, not realizing that everything in life requires
    proper learning; for example, we cannot become
    a neurosurgeon or achieve proficiency in music
    or become a black belt in martial arts by taking a
    weekend course.

3. **Procrastination.** What is procrastination?
    Unjustified postponement is called procrastination.
    Justified postponement is OK, unjustified is not.
    For example, when a doctor postpones writing the
    prescription because he is waiting for the blood
    report, that is justified. Unjustified postponement is
    when there is something I could do and should do,
    but I don't do it or I won't do it. 'Don't do' means
    I have a bad attitude, and 'won't do' means I am
    stubborn like a pig.

Procrastination is the enemy of progress.

**Keep in mind the greatest masters were the
greatest disasters when they started; they all
wanted to quit, but they didn't.**

How do you inculcate the habit of finishing what you start?

- **Stay focused, avoid distraction.** Staying focused is tough but rewarding, whereas getting distracted is easy but penalizing. Instead of finishing what is at hand, don't keep looking at new things.
- **Develop self-discipline.** It takes a lot of persistence and commitment to maintain self-discipline. Maintaining self-discipline is tough and painful in the short run but rewarding in the long run. Far-sighted people prefer short-term pain for long-term gain, whereas short-sighted people prefer short-term gain, not realizing it leads to long-term pain. Indiscipline is easy in the short run but painful in the long run.

You need self-discipline to finish what you start. Take the following actions:

1. Break your goals into small bites.
2. Track your progress with a timeline.
3. Hold yourself accountable to yourself and others.
4. Our objective is progress and not perfection.

If you are the kind of person who can see a project to completion, you always have an advantage over others. In life, results are rewarded, efforts are not.

Incomplete work drains energy because that never gives us a feeling of accomplishment. A completed project energizes, gives satisfaction and contentment and is relaxing.

Finishing strong is an everyday occurrence as there will never be a race, goal, day, quarter or year that does not come to an end. This means finishing strong is not an act, it's a habit.

Our greatest weakness lies in giving up instead of giving things one more shot.

Success is nothing more than practicing a few simple disciplines every day.

Winners never quit and quitters never win.

ACTIVITY

1. Identify one major take-home from this chapter.

    _____

    _____

    _____

2. Identify three areas in your life where you started something well but did not finish it.

    _____

    _____

    _____

3. I commit to practicing a new hobby for six weeks.

Stress could either propel us to go forward or prevent us from taking action.

7

Positive Stress

Any change or event whether positive or negative can cause stress. Stress can be good or bad, positive or negative. **Positive stress energizes and negative stress drains us**. Positive stress makes us perform better and achieve greater heights in life, and negative stress can bring ill health, frustration, confusion, etc.

Some examples of positive events:

- Vacation
- Childbirth
- Marriage in the family
- Graduation ceremony
- Starting a new job
- Promotion
- Buying your first home
- Buying a new car
- Asking someone on a date

Positive stress may bring gratification, meaning and happiness. Positive stress is perceived as an opportunity. Positive stress was termed 'eustress' by Dr. Hans Selye, author of *Stress without Distress*. Positive stress makes you uneasy, yet it gives you a feeling of comfort. Life without positive stress would just be boring. It could leave us unfulfilled or with wasted potential, which might in turn lead to depression or loss of self-esteem. Positive stress can spur us to take action and push us beyond our limits, prompting us to take risks that we normally might not. Hence, positive stress is crucial to fulfillment in our life.

Effects of Positive Stress

- Positive stress can be a great motivator. It energizes us and, when channelized, prevents complacence and enhances performance.
- It can push us to look at new options and open new doors. It can push us to step out of our comfort zone and make us achieve greater heights in life.
- It can help us overcome and relieve pressure.
- Stress can be seen as a motivator; it can help repair broken relationships.
- It teaches flexibility and adaptability, especially when things are beyond one's control. It makes us learn to accept things.
- It gives us the confidence to say no to unreasonable demands.
- Often, stress pushes us to arrive at a solution by analyzing the problem.
- Often, stress forces us to address a challenge immediately. Hence, it prevents us from procrastinating and prompts us to address the task at hand.
- It causes a person to focus on a particular challenge by triggering a fight-or-flight response.

Life without positive stress would be totally bland, dull and without any excitement.

ACTIVITY

1. Identify one major take-home from this chapter.

    _____

    _____

    _____

2. Identify an area of positive stress that makes you
    perform better.

    _____

    _____

    _____

Life is short. Don't make it shorter.

8

Negative Stress

Negative stress is called distress. Negative stress makes us frustrated, anxious, depressed, lethargic, drained out and sick. We do not feel good. A major consequence of this is loss of self-esteem.

When you perceive stress as a threat, it is termed negative stress. It makes you uneasy and gives you a feeling of discomfort. Negative stress makes a person go haywire and decreases their performance levels.

Effects of Negative Stress

Negative stress can be classified as physical, mental and emotional stress.

Physical stress could come from incidents such as bodily harm, mugging, a threat or a road accident.

Physical Symptoms of Stress

- Sleep disorder or insomnia
- Fatigue
- Indigestion
- Feeling sick
- Body ache

- Weight gain or loss
- High pulse rate
- High or low blood pressure
- Low energy levels
- Low immunity levels leading to frequent colds, coughs and infections
- Loss of sexual desire or ability or both
- Nervousness and tremors; ringing in the ears
- Cold hands and feet
- Excessive sweating
- Dry mouth

There are many more symptoms beyond the ones listed here.

Consequences of Negative Stress

Reports released by the United States' Substance Abuse and Mental Health Services Administration paint a scary picture.[6] If the state of the mental health of its people is an indicator of success, America is a land of suffering.

- Approximately 42 million adults are suffering from anxiety or other mental health disorders in America.
- Every year, doctors prescribe Valium for one out of every four Americans; this adds up to 60 million prescriptions a year.
- Emotional illnesses impact 25 to 50 percent of the population.
- Approximately 50 percent of marriages end in divorce.
- Some 60 to 80 percent accidents at work are stress related.

- About 70 percent of youth in juvenile detention centers have been diagnosed with a mental health disorder.

According to the Harvard Medical School, the three most common mental health disorders among women are:

- Depression
- Specific phobia, a disabling anxiety that interferes with daily life
- Post-traumatic stress disorder (PTSD)

The three most common mental health disorders among men are:

- Alcohol abuse
- Depression
- Specific phobia[7]

According to the World Health Organization (WHO), in 2019, close to one billion people were living with mental disorders, including anxiety and depression.[8]

According to Gallup, about 17 percent (44 million people) of Americans are being treated for depression.[9]

What a paradox that self-help books promising success and happiness are being purchased in the millions in such countries! Yet stress is preventing us from achieving success and happiness.

Emotional Symptoms of Negative Stress

- Irritation or agitation
- Frustration
- Impatience
- Nervousness
- Being preoccupied all the time

- Depression
- Loss of control: feeling hopeless and helpless
- Low self-esteem: feeling of inferiority or worthlessness
- Loss of sense of humor
- Loneliness and depression leading to a person being introverted and withdrawn
- Difficulty in overcoming mental turmoil
- Insecurity
- Indecisiveness
- Worry or tension
- Inability to concentrate or focus
- Procrastination
- Loss of memory
- Eating too much or too little
- Substance abuse
- Restlessness
- Withdrawal or sense of isolation
- Crying easily
- Mood swings

Stress is like a termite that eats a tree from the inside till it is destroyed.

ACTIVITY

1. Identify one major take-home from this chapter.

   _____

   _____

   _____

2. Are you suffering from any symptom of negative stress? If yes, what?

   _____

   _____

   _____

3. How do you plan to overcome it?

   _____

   _____

   _____

Stress comes from
both expecting
good things from
bad people and bad
things from good
people.

9

Causes of Stress

Stress can be caused by two factors: external or internal.

It is not uncommon for people to get trapped in a vicious cycle because of their inability to recognize the causes of stress. It is imperative to recognize the causes of stress and take timely, corrective action.

Stress Creators

External factors are beyond our control, such as traffic jams, road blockages, natural calamities and bad weather. We need to learn to live with these disruptions and accept them as a way of life.

Internal factors are related to our attitude and mindset. These can be changed and controlled. For example, a traffic jam is an external factor, but how we respond to the traffic jam is an internal factor. Is the traffic jam causing the stress or is it our attitude determining our response to the traffic jam? The examples of John and Steve in Chapter 1 demonstrate this very well.

We have to be conscious of what is causing us stress. Is it the event or is it our response to the event?

Sometimes an event does not even need to happen – just the thought of the event can be stressful. This means that something that occurred in the past or even the thought of it happening in the future could lead to stress. It would not be wrong to say that stress is the result of our mental conditioning.

- One cause of our stress is not being in control or not being in charge of our life, drifting and wandering helplessly and hopelessly.

  Unfulfilled expectations can also cause stress.

Stress related to work, family, social matters or finances could be our undoing and should be looked into properly. Poor relationships, traffic jams, children, parenting, travel, recreation, shopping, all can be causes of stress on an everyday basis. Some of these can easily be done away with.

- One major cause of stress is irrational thinking. Hence, changing our thinking process may help reduce stress. Most irrational beliefs come from our faulty upbringing and the media. Sometimes irrational beliefs are so deeply entrenched in us that it is a huge struggle for us to snap out of it. Irrational beliefs are not only hard to identify but also difficult to get rid of. They make us interpret situations in a negative manner, which may be totally uncalled for. To get rid of irrational beliefs we must start identifying them, and then take the steps to overcome them.

An irrational approach to decision-making and problem-solving could also lead to stress. Keep in mind that blowing a problem out of proportion amounts to inviting stress. Many times we make a mountain out of a molehill. We often find ourselves upset over minor things, for example, a casual remark by a colleague or spilling of coffee or water or a broken fingernail. In hindsight, our challenges, setbacks and disappointments often appear as a blessing to us.

The focus of this book is on getting rid of our irrational beliefs so we may lead happy, healthy, stress-free lives.

Most of us carry around some false beliefs which can be called irrational. Examples of irrational and rational beliefs are given below.

Irrational belief	Rational belief
I never do anything right	I do some things right, but I need to improve
I never reach anywhere on time	I am often late; I need to be on time
I will never get ahead in life	I plan to get ahead in life
I am not a creative person	I am working on improving my creativity
Nobody wants to be my friend	I need to learn how to make friends

Here are some other causes of stress.

Personal causes of stress could be

- Organizing birthday parties, weddings or vacations
- Moving house
- Work pressure, such as deadlines, distractions and poor performance
- Unresolved conflicts
- Death or divorce in the family

- Lack of priorities or bad life management
- Being disorganized
- Lack of time or impatience
- Lack of work–life balance
- Financial problems
- Misinterpretations or unrealistic expectations

Physical causes of stress could be

- Lack of physical fitness
- Biological changes brought about by puberty, pregnancy or diet
- Illness
- Unhealthy environment, for example, pollution

Emotional causes of stress could be

- Insecurity – personal and professional
- Not being in control
- Feeling of inferiority or insecurity
- Emotional imbalance
- Self-put-downs or negative self-talk
- False perception of ourself
- Blowing things out of proportion
- Misunderstandings
- Going against one's value system
- Incompetence
- Low self-esteem
- Lack of self-acceptance
- Feeling of being trapped or cornered
- Lack of focus
- Guilt and resentment
- Uncertainty
- Job concerns

- Inability to cope with change
- Unrealistic expectations
- Taking on more than we can handle
- Trying to please everybody all the time
- Pretending to be what we are not, putting on a mask or being hypocritical
- Unclear roles and goals in life
- Chronic worrier personality: some people worry even if everything is going alright, thinking something must be wrong somewhere, and are paranoid
- Negative thinking: some people keep thinking something wrong or bad is going to happen to the point of making it a self-fulfilling prophecy; in fact, they invite mishaps
- Phobias: for example, some people don't go for medical check-ups and think that if they go for a check-up, something wrong will come to light; they can't deal with their phobias
- False belief: some people are superstitious; for example, they do not make a will, thinking that if they do, they will die

Many causes of stress also become consequences. For example, poor performance is a cause of stress, but when a person is under stress, it leads to poor performance, whereby it becomes a consequence of stress. It is the same with health problems, lack of focus, conflicts and other causes. It becomes a vicious cycle.

Conflicting thoughts create turmoil and stress, whereas clarity relaxes or brings peace and calmness.

ACTIVITY

1. List three major challenges you are facing at home
    that are causing stress. Are they internal or external?

    _____

    _____

    _____

2. List three major challenges you are facing at work.
    Are they external or internal?

    _____

    _____

    _____

3. How do you plan to overcome these six challenges?

    _____

    _____

    _____

10

Stressors

Anxiety does not prepare us for a better tomorrow, but it certainly drains us of our strength today, making us more unprepared for tomorrow.

External Versus Internal Stressors

Stress causes psychological imbalances in our body when we encounter a threat, perceived or real. The key to tackling the pain is to first identify the pain point.

Examples of external stress factors that cannot be changed:

- Death of a loved one
- Unexpected natural disaster
- Political or economic situation: global or local
- Terminal illness of self or a loved one

To cope with external stress, we need to learn to accept that we cannot change circumstances or events beyond our control.

What we can do:

- Prepare for it
- Find a solution to circumvent it
- Build a coping mechanism

Internal stress factors are:
- Related to our fears
- Within our circle of influence

To cope with internal stress, we must:
- Avoid suffering by changing our perspective/ attitude
- Accept what cannot be changed

Stressors at Work

- Competition/conflicts with colleagues
- Environment (both internal and external)
- Indifferent behavior of colleagues
- Peer rivalry
- Dirty politics
- Scarce resources
- Deadlines
- Too much or too little work
- Lack of challenges
- Job insecurity
- Unpleasant or inadequate supervision
- Constant negative reprimand
- Mismatch of values
- Manipulative behavior
- Hypocritical/incompetent boss
- Lack of clarity of roles and goals
- Inadequate training
- Lack of rewards and recognition
- Lack of feeling of belonging
- Unrealistic expectations

Personal Stressors

External

Behavioral factors

- Conflict with friends or relatives
- Troubled relationships – breakup, trust issues, etc.
- Experiencing bullying or cultural/racial discrimination
- Inability to juggle multiple roles
- Lack of emotional support
- Personal loss due to death/divorce/breakup
- Problematic family dynamics – abusive relationships
- Financial distress or dependence
- Caregiver anxiety while parenting or caring for disabled family member
- Social media and technology – being affected by social comments or over-relying on technology

Psychological factors

- Past traumatic experiences

Physiological factors – unhealthy lifestyle

- Suffering from chronic illness
- Persistent physical discomfort due to constant pain, like in arthritis
- Insomnia or insufficient sleep due to overwork, resulting in fatigue and diminished mental agility
- Hormonal changes/imbalance
- Environment – constant exposure to pollutants/toxins
- Mental sluggishness
- Genetic predisposition to diseases such as cancer causing anticipatory stress

- Physical disability, leading to dependency on others

Internal

Psychological factors

- Inability to say no
- Psychological need to be liked by others
- Low self-esteem
- Constant critical evaluation of self or doubting one's ability
- Setting high standards for self, ignoring one's capabilities
- Oversensitivity to criticism
- Inability to accept one's improvement areas
- Getting defensive
- Poor time management
- Procrastination
- Lack of coping mechanisms or skills
- Overthinking – paralysis of analysis
- Feeling of lack of control over life or situations
- Feeling of inferiority
- Lack of confidence
- Fragile ego
- Inability to seek support due to psychological issues
- Lack of emotional intelligence or stability
- Ego issues or other psychological reasons leading to inflexible behavior and inability to adapt to new situations
- Excessive deliberation – constantly replaying negative events and overthinking
- Pessimistic view of life – negative thinking

- Perfectionist attitude
- Work-related pressures
- Overreacting

Physiological factors – unhealthy lifestyle

- Sleep deprivation and insomnia
- Overindulgence in socializing
- Drug/alcohol abuse
- Excessive workout regime

Feelings of guilt and resentment drain more energy than hard work could ever do.

ACTIVITY

1. List three examples of stressful situations at work.

   _____

   _____

   _____

2. How do you plan to overcome these situations?

   _____

   _____

   _____

3. List three behaviors that stem from your personal and social life which lead to stressful situations.

   _____

   _____

   _____

4. How do you plan to overcome these behaviors?

   _____

   _____

   _____

The responsibility of handling stress cannot be delegated.

11

Handling Stress

Why is stress management important?

Work-related stress leads to a loss of more than $300 billion a year because of absenteeism, health issues and lower productivity. This loss can be prevented or at least brought down significantly.[10]

Millions of people live in constant fear of losing their jobs due to downsizing, restructuring or the adoption of new technologies among others. Since most people spend many hours at work every day, stress management should become a way of life. Significantly, nearly 50 percent of large companies in the United States provide some type of stress management training for their workforce.[11]

Just the way a computer is not manufactured to fail, human beings are not engineered to fail either. People with even a basic familiarity with computers know two things:

- To successfully operate a computer, they must read the instructions carefully.
- In spite of reading the user manual carefully, they will need the help of an expert to understand some instructions.

Good instructions that have stood the test of time can be the differentiating factor between success and failure in all areas of life.

Why are instruction manuals important? Because they are meant to prevent you from making mistakes and having accidents.

Under stress, we feel rushed and frustrated, and it seems we go from one crisis to another. **Once in a while we all can handle stress, but on a permanent basis, it starts taking its toll.** Our body and nervous system start breaking down. The wear and tear is extraordinary. The body starts generating harmful chemicals, which in turn weaken our immune system, leading to illnesses and premature aging.

We all want to achieve new heights, but there is something pulling us down. And what is that something? It is stress. **Imagine trying to accelerate a car with the brakes on. The car engine would get damaged and blow up.** Similarly, stress prevents us from achieving our purpose. We need to identify and understand what is pulling us down. We need to get rid of that and then go back to accelerating to achieve success.

One cannot live life frivolously. In spite of so many stress relief remedies and devices, why is there still so much stress? The answer is very simple. Most of those remedies address the symptoms and not the cause. Nor do we consciously try to get rid of the negative habits and the mindset that cause stress.

Isn't it time that we take charge of our lives and stop the insanity immediately?

Doctors say that 50–75 percent of sickness or illness is psychosomatic – 'psyche' being the mind and 'soma' being the body. Sickness gets manifested in the body because of the psyche – the mind.

In the 1980s, physicians saw an increase in patients with stress-related issues. The trend continues to this day.

Did you know that antidepressants are among the most prescribed drugs in the world? According to the Daily Health Post, April 14, 2015, **'Between 1994 and 2008, the use of antidepressants increased by a staggering 400%.'**

Somehow, people are not paying enough attention to the causes of stress and address only the symptoms instead of finding the true meaning of life.

People get up every day and battle with emptiness and loneliness just to survive. When life holds no meaning, people don't know what to do or where to go. They are confused. They fall prey to empty advice: 'Why don't you do this, and why don't you do that?' In such situations, people feel a loss of control. They live in constant fear. They only hear scary voices from the past. They don't find any sense of self-worth or meaning. They end up making wrong choices, not realizing that they are the contributors to the mess in their life.

Unmanaged stress is a major challenge in most people's lives.

When we experience too much change in a short period, we feel uncomfortable and fear a loss of control. Such perception contributes to enhancing stress. Sometimes coping involves adjusting to unusual demands, and it may require more effort and energy than when we are in a state of equilibrium.

Prolonged emotional discomfort can lead to high levels of stress and eventually to physical breakdown. What can we do to protect ourselves against prolonged stress? The most important strategy would be to maintain emotionally supportive relationships. Such strong emotional relationships act as a buffer against the negative impact of stress.

Experience shows that coping is a process rather than an event. Different people use different coping mechanisms or multiple strategies at different times.

Reactions to Stress

- **Denial:** People who live in denial don't realize that facts do not go away just by ignoring them. They are living in a fool's paradise. They adopt the ostrich approach. They tend to bury their heads in the sand thinking that if they see no danger, there is no danger. They avoid confrontation, resulting in damaging consequences. How foolish and self-deceptive they are!
- **Indifferent attitude:** People who are indifferent have a non-caring attitude or 'I don't care' attitude. Indifference does not mean that danger is not there. They are inviting trouble. This is a recipe for disaster.
- **Escapist behavior:** People with an escapist behavior don't have the guts to face up to the situation. They keep postponing addressing the problem, not realizing that the more they postpone, the more they compound the problem, and the price to pay becomes higher. People with an escapist attitude often become self-abusive.

They take refuge in drugs, alcohol, smoking and other vices. They justify this by saying things like 'Alcohol soothes my nerves', 'Smoking relaxes me' and 'Drugs make me forget my problems'. What is this if not self-abuse? If you respect yourself, would you abuse yourself? Besides, through this escapist behavior, does the problem get minimized or eliminated? Certainly not! In fact, it snowballs into a bigger problem because the escapist becomes weaker. Escapist behavior is different from addiction, but if we are not careful, escapist behaviors can be gateways to addictions.

- **Taking it out on a third party:** It is not unusual that the person under stress because of emotional imbalance takes out his anger on a third party, thereby compounding his problem. People throw a fit when they are stressed. This is like killing the messenger who is carrying bad news. By doing this, does the problem get resolved? It doesn't. It remains where it was.

- **Being proactive and responding:** Address or remove the cause. The most mature way to handle stress is to identify the causes and address them. If professional help is required, one should seek it. We need to learn to handle stress before our health suffers, our family breaks down or we lose our jobs. Delay is a luxury that no one can afford. Negative stress needs to be destroyed before it destroys us.

Benefits of Handling Stress Effectively

- Builds immunity
- Improves health

- Reduces sickness and disease
- Creates a happier lifestyle
- Increases productivity or output
- Improves motivation and morale
- Helps build better and strong relationships at home and at work
- Increases ability to focus or concentrate
- Improves clarity of thought
- Gives you more energy
- Spurs self-confidence and self-esteem
- Leaves you feeling good
- Leads to better quality of life
- Spurs positive thinking and positive energy, leading to positive action
- Improves your ability to channelize energy productively
- Leads to better problem-solving ability
- Helps you make better decisions and take more decisive actions
- Enhances your ability to handle unpleasant situations effectively
- Helps you stay creative and solution-focused
- Enhances your risk-taking ability

Positive habits accelerate us to success; negative habits pull us down.

ACTIVITY

1. Identify one major take-home from this chapter.

     _____

     _____

     _____

2. As a rule, do you respond to stress proactively? Identify an area of improvement in your life.

     _____

     _____

     _____

3. I commit to changing the following behavior:

     _____

     _____

There are people who blow things out of proportion.
A broken nail could be painful but does not call for a third world war.

12

Steps to Handle Stress

Is it possible to stay relaxed when you are faced with threats? Is it possible to face challenges of life with serenity and calmness? Imagine waking up every day with confidence, ready to tackle whatever life throws at you. Picture yourself mastering the art of staying cool and calm in the face of life's trials and tribulations.

We all possess the power to decide our responses to life's challenges. We need to cultivate resilience and develop inner peace. It is not what happens to us but how we respond to it that matters.

Here are constructive and destructive ways of handling stress.

Constructive	Destructive
• Swimming	• Overeating
• Jogging	• Smoking
• Going for a walk	• Drinking alcohol
• Deep breathing	• Getting violent
• Taking a bath	• Throwing things
• Practicing yoga	• Harming oneself
• Getting a massage	• Not showing up at work
• Watching a funny movie	• Yelling at your kids
• Gardening	

Constructive	Destructive
• Painting	• Watching too much TV
• Knitting	• Taking narcotics
• Reading a book	• Punching things
• Listening to relaxing music	• Eating junk food
• Aerobic exercise	• Shouting at others
• Meditation	• Overspending
• Thought restructuring	
• Stretching	
• Muscle relaxation	

Dealing with stress in a constructive way makes you feel good right away and has long-term benefits. Adopting bad or destructive ways of dealing with stress may produce short-term pleasantness but has hurtful long-term effects.

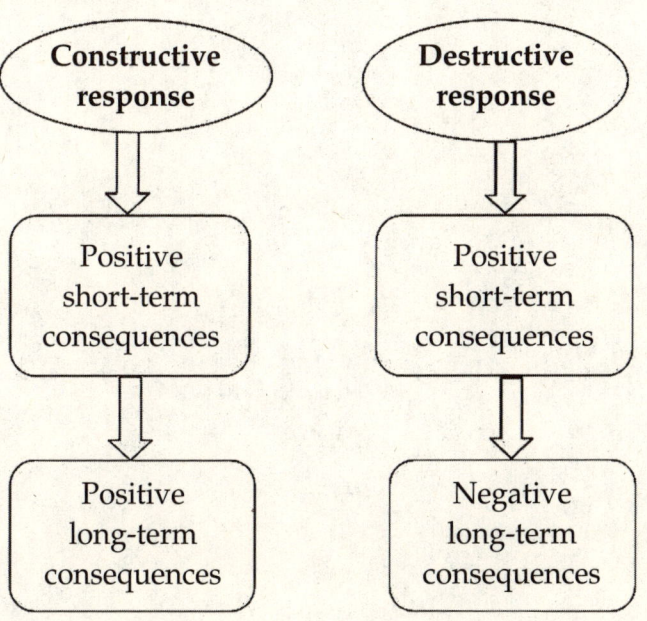

Stress cannot be avoided, but we need to develop healthy mechanisms to either prevent it or cope with it. Prevention is better than cure.

People with foresight preempt and prevent problems. Short-sighted people only do postmortems.

ACTIVITY

1. List some constructive ways in which you handle stress.

    _____

    _____

    _____

2. List some destructive ways in which you handle stress.

    _____

    _____

    _____

3. How can you avoid using destructive ways of handling stress?

    _____

    _____

    _____

4. I commit to adopting the following constructive ways of handling stress:

    _____

    _____

    _____

SMALL changes produce BIG outcomes.

13

The Small Change Principle

Small investments today can lead to a very profitable tomorrow. Small changes have a ripple effect.

Research shows that most diets don't work. Most people who lose weight gain back the same or even more within a matter of months. It appears that the only sustainable way to stay away from weight gain is to make very small, sustainable changes in one's eating and exercising habits.[12]

Experience shows that only 10 percent of issues are responsible for employee burnout. In other words, small adjustments can affect significant change.

There was a lady who was stressed out and decided that she would get up ten minutes earlier than usual every morning. She used these ten minutes to have a cup of tea and relax. Initially, it seemed quite insignificant, but as time went by, she noticed her days were relaxed, her relationships improved and her productivity went up. It was a small change that made a big difference.

***

John had been working as an office manager for five years. But gradually he started hating his job; he felt that he was being treated unfairly and was being blamed for everything that went wrong. He had to make many trips to the photocopier every day; this meant he was using his time unproductively, and it became an irritant for him. John's supervisor was mature; he arranged for a small photocopier solely for John, which was placed within easy reach. This small change brought about a big difference.

***

Steve was a general manager at a large corporation with its parent office in the UK. He was frustrated, because he felt that nobody trusted him. He had to seek approvals from the corporate office for every expenditure over $1,000. He requested that the policy be reviewed, and in light of his past record his limit should be increased to $3,000. The message was conveyed to Steve's boss, who found out that Steve was responsible for 50 people and a million-dollar budget. The boss approved the $3,000 limit, and thereafter everything went smoothly. In Steve's case, a small change made a big difference.

It's a lot easier to change 1 percent in a hundred different areas than to change 100 percent in any one area.

ACTIVITY

1. How can small changes be used to prevent burnouts?

    _____

    _____

    _____

2. What is the small change principle? Give examples.

    _____

    _____

    _____

3. Identify a small change that can lead to a big outcome in your office.

    Small change   **Big outcome**
    _____

    _____

4. Identify a small change that can lead to a big outcome at home.

    Small change   **Big outcome**

    _____

14

Learn to Forgive and Forget

Haven't we all been hurt by the actions or words of another person? What about a traumatic experience of being abused physically or emotionally by someone close to you? Such wounds can leave feelings of resentment, bitterness, anger and even hatred for a long time.

Some of us feel that holding on to things makes us strong, not realizing that sometimes it is letting go that makes us stronger. Forgiveness is a conscious decision to let go of resentment and anger. We cannot erase or undo the action, but forgiveness can lessen the emotional scars. It does not mean overlooking or ignoring the harm done to you, nor does it mean reconciliation with the person who hurt you. Forgiveness is like a settlement that works as damage control to help you get on with life.

There is a lot of value in forgiving and forgetting. Even for a selfish reason it makes sense. Forgiveness is like emancipation, gaining freedom from a self-imposed burden. Forgiveness reduces stress and gives us peace of mind.

Letting go of bitterness can bring peace of mind and lead to benefits:

- Better mental and physical health
- Less stress and anxiety
- Improved relationships
- Strong immunity
- Better self-esteem

Often we hear people say, '**I can forgive, but I cannot forget.**' It is not unusual to see siblings have. Often, they stop talking to each other. That bitterness continues from one generation to the next.

Bill and Harry were childhood friends, but something happened and their relationship fell apart. They did not talk to each other for twenty-five years. Harry was critically ill and hospitalized. Bill thought, 'Life is too short, why don't I become the bigger person and forgive and forget.' He went to see Harry in the hospital. They caught up after twenty-five years. After three hours, Bill wished Harry a speedy recovery and said, 'It's getting late, I have to go.' They said their final goodbyes. But before Bill reached the door, Harry shouted from his bed, 'Bill, in case I don't die, this forgiveness doesn't count.' What was Harry saying? 'I can forgive but I cannot forget.'

Why do we hold a grudge? When someone we trust hurts us, it causes anger, sadness and frustration. If we dwell on the hurtful situation, it causes bitterness or depression. Grudges can destroy relationships.

Stop holding grudges. Whenever we hold on to a grudge, who are we hurting the most? Invariably, ourselves. Holding grudges is like carrying excess baggage – you have to pay a price for it. Most of the time the price comes in the form of ill health or sickness, and the other person may not even know that you exist. Holding a grudge is like an acid that corrodes the utensil it is in.

What if I am the one who needs forgiveness?

Forgiveness starts with oneself. Often we keep punishing ourselves, much more than anyone else ever punishes us, by retaining guilt and resentment. There is no person in the world who does not make mistakes. If you know someone who has never made a mistake in life, then you know someone who has never done anything anyway. Making a mistake is not the end of the world but realizing and repeating it is.

We need to accept that we are not perfect. I have my pluses and minuses. I am not proud of my mistakes. I learned from my mistakes. I seek forgiveness for my mistakes. I apologize for my mistakes. **I made a mistake, but I am not a mistake**.

Forgiving oneself is important to move on. By not forgiving yourself, how long do you keep punishing yourself? Until death! Shouldn't there be a cut-off point in life?

Being kind to yourself is not selfishness – it is necessary. If we cannot forgive ourselves, how can we forgive others in this world? We can only give what we have. How can we give what we don't have?

Once you realize your mistake, apologize immediately and emphatically. Don't be defensive. **An apology does not always mean that you are wrong, it only means that you value your relationship more than your ego.**

Forgive and forget sounds wonderful in theory, but it is not easy to achieve. And there is a fine distinction here. What if the person who hurt you does not realize his mistakes or admit to them? It is well said you cheat me once, shame on you; you cheat me twice, shame on me. Forgiveness beyond a point is self-destruction.

Some people seek forgiveness because they mean it, whereas some people seek forgiveness to buy time. For those who genuinely mean it, a sincere apology is a way of making amends and starting afresh with a clean record. However, some apologies are so shallow that they have the opposite effect. We need to learn to judge people based on their actions and not words.

Forgiving the habitual defaulter is not magnanimity but stupidity.

ACTIVITY

1. Identify one major take-home from this chapter.

   _____

   _____

   _____

2. Identify an area in life where you are holding a grudge or feeling resentful against yourself or someone else.

   _____

   _____

   _____

3. How do you plan to use the principle 'to forgive and forget'?

   _____

   _____

   _____

15

Be Flexible
Through Adversities

Life is unpredictable. Sometimes it throws you a curveball such as loss of a job, breakup, failing a venture or even bad weather, which can be challenging to handle. It is normal and natural to feel dejected in the face of such adversities. But we have to learn to roll with the punches.

Challenges are a reality of life – they test our inner strength.

Jane was preparing to host a nice outdoor birthday party for her son. She diligently put up all the decorations and laid out the food. But without warning the sky became overcast, and it rained. Question is, did she create the rain? Did she have any control over the situation? No. But she had a choice: either to get mad and ruin everybody's mood or to move indoors and salvage whatever she could. The purpose was to get together and enjoy.

Every hurdle needs to be converted into a stepping stone.

ACTIVITY

1. Identify one major take-home from this chapter.

   _____

   _____

   _____

2. Think of a similar situation in your life where you could have handled an adversity better by being more flexible.

   _____

   _____

   _____

3. I commit to making the following change in my life:

   _____

   _____

   _____

16

Think Outside the Box

Don't blow problems out of proportion. Remember, you are not the only person in the world to have problems. Someone, somewhere in the world, has faced similar or worse problems before.

Don't complicate things.

Once a man went to a psychiatrist and said, 'Doc, I can't sleep properly. I am scared. I always feel that someone is under my bed, and they will come and catch me.' The psychiatrist said, 'No problem, I will cure you of your phobia. Just come to me for thirty sessions. Each session will cost you a thousand dollars.' The man said, 'I will think about it and get back.' But he never went back.

Six months later the doctor ran into this man at a shopping mall and asked, 'Why didn't you come back?' The patient said, 'I have cured myself completely.' The doctor asked, 'How did you do it?' The patient said, 'I shared my problem with a friend, and he immediately gave me a solution which I implemented, and the problem went away. The solution was to chop the legs off the bed so that there was no gap between the bed and the floor. So nobody could hide there. I have been enjoying a relaxed and comfortable sleep ever since. What's more, with the money I would have paid you I bought a new car.'

Sometimes the solutions are genuinely simple and the problems may be psychological. Our mind is like a mirror – it only reflects; it does not react. A mirror simply reflects what's in front of it. Similarly, we can be like a mirror. Whenever something goes wrong or something stressful happens, we must take a step back, look at ourselves objectively as an observer, without getting entangled. Objectivity and detachment do not amount to indifference. Rather, this attitude is about maintaining peace of mind and calmness in a stressful situation. How we handle adverse situations every day is a choice, such as responding to a rude comment or discourteous behavior, traffic jams, a battle of words or any crisis. These are situations that test the maturity of one's mind. We cannot control other people's behavior or what life throws at us, but we can choose our response.

Choosing calmness over chaos is a conscious response. **Calmness is a choice.** Ask yourself whether the situation is worth getting upset over or worth losing your peace of mind. Harness the power of visualization by responding in a calm and rational manner. With practice, it becomes a habit, and eventually positive behavior becomes permanent. This shift is a powerful, life-changing tool. If used wisely, it can transform our lives – not because the world has changed but because we have changed.

Choosing calmness over chaos does not mean denying our emotions but managing them in a way that gives us control and peace of mind.

ACTIVITY

1. Identify one major take-home from this chapter.

   _____

   _____

   _____

2. Think of a time when you blew a problem out of proportion. What was it?

   _____

   _____

   _____

3. How would you handle it today?

   _____

   _____

   _____

17

High Self-Esteem of a Winner

What is self-esteem? Self-esteem is a feeling of self-worth. Just like air, high self-esteem is essential for survival. It empowers a person and reflects in their every action. It is the foundation stone of the psyche on which our behavior rests. It is an acceptance of our own intrinsic value.

Self-esteem is the way we feel about ourselves. When we feel good, the world looks nice, our productivity goes up and our relationships are a lot better. And the opposite is just as true.

The foundation of self-esteem lies in self-acceptance. What does that mean? It means that you can confidently say, 'I accept myself the way I am.' Self-acceptance doesn't mean complacence or arrogance. Self-acceptance does not mean saying, 'That's the way I am' and 'That's the way I will be'. 'If you don't like it, too bad, take it or leave it' amounts to arrogance. Properly understood and analyzed, self-esteem is the epitome of humility. It is based on the following beliefs:

- I have no idea how I came into this world – it's a mystery, but I am here, and I'm here to stay.

- By no standards am I perfect.

None of us is perfect. There are certain things we are born with such as our height, skin color and the shape of our face. They may not be ideal. Some of these characteristics are beyond our control, that is, we didn't create them, nor can we change them. Maybe we can try to improve some of these to an extent, but we cannot do away with them. In such a case, we can either keep fighting what we cannot change or accept them as part of our identity and build on them.

Lack of acceptance of ourselves as we are creates an identity crisis. Identity crisis is the beginning of all problems. The moment we practice self-acceptance, we overcome our internal turmoil and are at peace with ourselves. We feel complete and adequate. We don't have to prove anything to anyone in the world. Self-acceptance gives us our own identity. We're not looking for validation from outside, which means we are internally driven, not externally.

For example, supposing one day a friend wakes up in a great mood, calls me up and says, 'What a great job you are doing, sharing a positive message on social responsibility with people.' I know he is sincere. How does it make me feel? Wonderful. But the next day he gets up in a rotten mood and calls me and says, 'You rascal, you cheat, you crook, you are the biggest fraud going on in town.' How would it make me feel? Rotten. Who is controlling my life? Another person. Is that the way I want to live? Absolutely not.

Folks, don't get me wrong. The first day when he calls me and says 'you are the greatest guy', it feels good, but if he doesn't say it, in my own eyes I am still a good human being. Why? Because I get validation from inside.

This is not arrogance; this is called being internally driven not externally. It means I am at peace with myself.

A person who is comfortable in his own skin needs no external validation.

Let me share with you a story I heard from a speaker. I am unable to authenticate it, but it makes a point.

Once Charlie Chaplin participated in a Charlie Chaplin lookalike competition without disclosing his identity. Guess what, he lost. He started thinking, what a world it is. The real one loses and the fake one wins. He thought, 'Should I disclose my identity?' He started thinking, 'Why should I do it? I know who I am, I know my identity, why do I have to prove anything to anyone?' He just walked away.

The way I see it, this is a great example of self-acceptance, without needing any validation from outside.

Your relationships with others are dependent on your relationship with yourself.

ACTIVITY

1. Identify one major take-home from this chapter.

    _____

    _____

    _____

2. Recall a time when you had low self-esteem.

3. What would you do differently now?

    _____

    _____

    _____

4. Make a list of your strengths and weaknesses. Why? Winners recognize their weaknesses but focus on their strengths. Losers recognize their strengths but focus on their weaknesses. Unless we know our strengths and weaknesses, how can we build on our strengths and overcome our weaknesses?

Strengths _____ **Weaknesses** _____

_____

Caring is positive
but pleasing for the
sake of appeasement
is negative.

18

Appeasement

The biggest cause of stress is trying to please everybody all the time. Trying to please everybody all the time is neither possible nor required. The desire to be likeable drives us to seek approval. Trying to seek approval all the time is not sustainable. The following story says it all.

Once a man and his son were going to the market with their donkey. They were both walking beside the donkey when a villager commented, 'Look at the fools, they have a donkey, yet they are walking.' The man lifted his son and put him on the donkey. But soon another villager passed by and said, 'Look at the shameless boy, sitting on a donkey and making his father walk.' So the boy got off the donkey and made his father sit on it. Another man who was passing by said, 'Look at the selfish man, sitting on a donkey and making his son walk.' At this point, both father and son didn't know what to do so they both got on the donkey. Another man commented that father and son should be ashamed of themselves for overloading the donkey. Finally, the father decided to tie the donkey to a pole and carry it to the market. As they were crossing the river, the donkey felt uncomfortable. It struggled hard and managed to free itself, but it fell into the river and drowned.

Rather than trying to please everybody all the time, we need to focus on finding our own path. Another form of appeasement is permanent approval-seeking behavior.

Permanent approval-seeking behavior shows two things:

- Lack of confidence
- You consider other people's opinions higher than your own

Consultation is positive but permanent approval-seeking is not.

This world is full of different people with different personalities, values, whims and fancies. People have demands, sometimes reasonable, sometimes not so. To begin with, it is pointless adding stress to your life. Remember, no matter what you do or say, someone will have a negative response. Do not take it personally. It is not unusual for people to criticize others when they are unhappy with their own lives. Keep in mind you do not need other people's approval to be happy.

Not trying to please does not mean that a person should have a callous or a non-caring attitude. Accept that it takes all kinds of people to make the world.

A friend to all is a friend to none.

ACTIVITY

1. Identify one major take-home from this chapter.

   _____

   _____

   _____

2. Have you ever gone out of your way to please someone to your detriment?

   _____

   _____

   _____

3. How would you change this behavior in the future?

   _____

   _____

   _____

19

Be Assertive

We should learn to say no and be assertive.

Assertive is when you feel strongly about something and have the courage to stand **firmly** but **politely**. The two words are important: firmness and politeness. They go together.

The moment you take politeness out of firmness, it becomes aggressiveness.

You have to respond assertively to discourteous remarks and insults even if only to maintain your sanity. One may not always be able to resolve an issue but getting it off your chest can relieve pressure. And this must be done in a calm and composed manner.

Quite often in offices too much work is dumped on one person because that person is too meek to say no. Work piles up and the incomplete work stresses him out. What if this person was assertive and clarified the quantum of work while setting boundaries. The question is, would that relieve his stress? The answer is yes. However, sometimes we need to stretch.

Once when I was running my leadership program, the following example came up.

Suppose you are waiting in line for a ticket. There are nine people ahead of you. Someone just comes from nowhere and goes straight to the ticket counter and says, 'Could you please give me my ticket first?' An assertive person would walk up and say, 'Sir, I am number ten and I would request you to kindly join the line.' Invariably, the other nine people will support you. However, if they don't, and if this person does not move, you go back and join the line. At least you will feel good that you had the courage to ask the person to join the line.

Once, an elderly principal of a school who attended my program stopped me and said, 'You call this assertiveness?' I said, 'Yes.' He said, 'I don't think so. What have you achieved? Nothing.' I asked him, 'Sir, then what do you call assertiveness?' He said, 'I will tell the other nine people that if he is number one then I am number two.' I asked the class how many of them agreed with the principal's approach. Some people disagreed. When they were asked what was the reason for their disagreement, they said, 'Two wrongs don't make a right.' Some people even said, 'What is the difference between me and the other person? We will overlook and maintain the status quo.' The principal was asked his reasoning. He replied:

1. *I am a law-abiding citizen. I obeyed the law. He is breaking the law. Who destroys our society? Never the activity of rascals but always the inactivity of the good people. If I remain silent, am I not encouraging him to do the wrong thing?*

2. *I could have a death in my family or someone in my family could need blood urgently, who are they to throw me from ten to eleven to twelve to thirteen? Who are they?*

Suppose more people kept breaking the queue like this, and you keep getting thrown behind. I want to ask the person who said I will maintain the status quo, how long will you tolerate being pushed further backwards? Will there be a time when you will walk up and say, 'Stop, enough is enough'? He may say yes, supposing that that time comes at number eighteen. Now tell us:

1. *You said two wrongs don't make a right, but how come eighteen wrongs make it right?*
2. *Whatever you do at number eighteen, why would you not do it at number ten?*

Often we act noble to hide our cowardice, not having the courage to stand up. The principal added, 'Of course, if there was a disabled person or a woman with two little kids crying or an elderly person or someone whose emergency is bigger than mine and he told me about it, I will let them go first. But not otherwise.'

Don't let others push you around.

Being courteous and positive does not mean that others can walk all over you. Learning to be assertive is crucial.

In fact, not being assertive or taking a stand can be a sign of weakness and encourages others to abuse you. It will invite disrespect. Many times being assertive is both necessary and unavoidable. Choices have to be made between principles and popularity.

Don't invite stress. Remember, you are not a shock absorber for the world's problems. Don't agree to terms that you disagree with just out of politeness. **Learn the art of disagreeing without being disagreeable.**

It is bad to abuse others but worse to let others abuse you.

ACTIVITY

1. Identify one major take-home from this chapter.

   _____

   _____

   _____

2. Identify a situation where you should have been assertive but were not.

   _____

   _____

   _____

3. How will you handle a similar situation in the future?

   _____

   _____

   _____

20

Face Things Head On

We must address issues and not push them under the rug. Be proactive and address issues instead of avoiding them. By ignoring facts, facts do not go away. They become worse.

Some people practice the ostrich approach. But this approach is ineffective as in reality the problem only gets compounded when it goes unattended. It becomes stronger and harder to handle.

Face up to the situation. We can live with the known; we cannot live with the unknown.

Twenty-five years ago a barium X-ray of my gastrointestinal tract showed a shadow in the area of the appendix. The doctors were confused and didn't know what it was. They did the X-ray again three months later and the shadow was gone. It became a bigger mystery now. The test was repeated three months later and the shadow appeared again. The doctors were puzzled. The doctor recommended an exploratory surgery. After taking a second opinion, I asked what the purpose of the surgery was, and the doctor said, 'We need to know what's going on – we can live with the known but not with the unknown.' Identifying the problem makes it a lot easier to find a solution. Upon diagnosis at least the doctor knows what to treat rather than just guessing. Upon surgery they found that the appendix was swollen, and it was not allowing the adjoining area to fill up. Hence it was appearing as a shadow.

Not knowing or suspense only brings stress and prolongs anxiety. It drains a person physically and mentally.

It is said that time is a big healer. Not always.

If we have a sepsis in our body or an infection, it will be foolhardy to say, 'I don't want to take any treatment because with time it will heal itself.' Obviously, it will not. It will spread much faster and poison your body. Inaction is a passive action or action by default, which only aggravates the situation. Many times, we have to face up to the situation and overcome it.

Just by ignoring facts, facts do not go away.

ACTIVITY

1. Identify one major take-home from this chapter.

   _____

   _____

   _____

2. Identify an area in life which is causing you stress
   but you are unwilling to address it.

   _____

   _____

   _____

3. How do you plan to overcome this?

   _____

   _____

   _____

Live by the philosophy of prepare and prevent rather than repair and repent.

21

Prepare and Prevent, Don't Repair and Repent

Prevention is better than cure. As the saying goes, the greatest fire in the world could have been prevented with one cup of water at the right time. Far-sighted people preempt and prevent problems.

- If you treat people with courtesy, you are preventing conflict.
- If you take pride in your performance, you will avoid making mistakes.
- If you teach positive values to children, you are protecting them from pitfalls.
- If you brush your teeth, you are preventing cavities.
- If you exercise, you are preventing illness.
- If you eat nutritious food, you are preventing ill health.
- If you wear seat belts in cars, you will prevent injury if you meet with an accident.

Our car needs servicing every few months, and we need to change the oil and filter periodically. Such preventive maintenance is done before breakdown. It increases the efficiency and productive life of the car. The chances of a breakdown reduce and effectiveness goes up.

The big question is, what is different about human beings? Don't our bodies and minds need preventive maintenance to avoid breakdown and repair?

Far-sighted people live by the philosophy of prepare and prevent rather than repair and repent.

ACTIVITY

1. Identify one major take-home from this chapter.

   _____

   _____

   _____

2. Identify an area in your life where you could use the philosophy of prepare and prevent rather than repair and repent.

   _____

   _____

   _____

3. How do you plan to implement it?

   _____

   _____

   _____

22

Get Your Priorities Right

We must learn to prioritize. The number of time-saving devices we have today is the highest we have ever had, and yet we don't have time. What a paradox! This is because somewhere we messed up our priorities. We forgot to distinguish between what's urgent and what's important in life.

Urgent may or may not be important and important may or may not be urgent. But what is interesting is that whenever we ignore what is important, it becomes urgent. For example, health is important. Exercising every day is important, but it's not urgent. If I have a crucial meeting tonight and I cannot exercise, it's not the end of the world. But if I ignore my health for long, undoubtedly I will land up in a hospital. Similarly, relationships are important, not urgent. But if we ignore relationships long enough, we start talking through our lawyers.

Lack of priorities destabilizes a person's life; it brings insecurity. At least 40 percent of our time should go into achieving important and long-term goals. Priorities should be chalked out and worked upon diligently.

A professor wanted to demonstrate the importance of setting priorities. Once the class settled down, he picked up a jar and filled it to the top with small rocks of about 2 inches in diameter. He asked the students if the jar was full. They all said yes. The professor poured into the jar a box of pebbles, again all the way to the top. The pebbles filled up the space in between the rocks. He asked again if the jar was full. The students said yes. The professor then took a box of sand and poured it into the jar. Of course the sand made space for itself and filled up all the empty spaces. Again, the professor asked if the jar was full. The answer again was yes. Next, he poured a glass of water into the jar. The water seeped down into the jar. Again, the professor asked if the jar was full. The students answered yes.

The professor said, 'I want you to remember this lesson forever. Realize that in your life the rocks are the most important part, which is your values, your family and your health. If they are lost, then you will be lost. The pebbles are the smaller, nice things to have, such as your job, your house and your car. The sand is the small stuff, insignificant with respect to the other things. Water if it can be accommodated is good; if not, it is insignificant.

Remember the 'jar theory'. You should fill up the jar with big rocks first and then fit in the smaller, less important or inconsequential things.

If you put the pebbles and the sand in the jar first, there will be no room for the rocks, which are the most important things in your life. The same is true as we go through life. If you spend all your energy on the small stuff, you will never have room for the most important things in life. No matter how full your jar is, there is still space for water in it but not at the cost of the more important things.

Moral of the story: first take care of those things which are the most important in life.

Here are five top priorities in life:

1. Good health
2. Good relationships
3. Confidence/self-improvement
4. Money
5. Balance of body, mind and soul

In my program, often I ask the participants, why do you go to work? The answer is, for the family. Why do they work hard? Again they say, for the family. Who are the most important people in their lives? They say family. Who are the most neglected people in their lives? Also the family. How sad that sometimes the most important people also become the most neglected people.

Certainly, I am guilty, and I am sure many of us are.

Lack of direction, not lack of time, is the problem.

Living with priorities helps us focus on what truly matters, ensuring we live our lives aligned with our values and goals.

Priorities in life act as a compass that navigates us to our destination.

When everything is a priority, then nothing is.

ACTIVITY

1. Identify one major take-home from this chapter.

   _____

   _____

   _____

2. Identify the three most important priorities in your life.

   _____

   _____

   _____

3. When was the last time you attended to these?

   _____

   _____

   _____

4. I commit to changing the following behavior:

   _____

   _____

   _____

23

Live Purposefully

Set little-little, small daily goals. Most people live aimlessly. They wake up in the morning, do their chores, go to work, come home in the evening tired, watch TV and go to sleep. This is the real world. Such people live a meaningless life. They die before they are dead. They only exist and never start living.

Live a purposeful life. Purpose gives meaning to life. It is a destination we want to reach. A lifetime goal is called a purpose. How do you define your purpose? Supposing you were age hundred today and were to look back at your life, what would you want to say is your accomplishment? That's your purpose. All our goals, whether short-term, mid-term or long-term, should lead us to our purpose. It's called alignment.

Your daily goals could be physical, financial or spiritual. Set daily goals for your physical exercise. Remember the saying 'by the inch, it's a cinch, but by the yard, it's hard'. How do you eat an elephant? One bite at a time. Consistency is more important than overdoing erratically. If you do not direct your life, then someone else will. If you do not have your own goals, then you automatically become part of other people's goals. It is true that all goals have a deadline, but living from one deadline to the next all your life can become very stressful. The answer lies in being cognizant that your goals are synchronized to avoid stress.

A purposeful life is a life full of purpose.

ACTIVITY

1. Identify one major take-home from this chapter.

   _____

   _____

   _____

2. Identify your purpose in life.

   _____

   _____

   _____

3. Identify your one-year, three-year and five-year goals that will help you attain your purpose in life.

   _____

   _____

   _____

24

Unrealistic Expectations Versus Reality

Evaluate your expectations. We are all guilty of having unrealistic expectations at some time or the other in life. Does being optimistic always guarantee a positive outcome in life, whether we are looking for a job or a boost in career or relationships? Maybe not, but being optimistic helps us better navigate life, especially in situations that are out of our control. However, there is a difference between being optimistic and having unrealistic expectations.

Stress is caused when there is a difference between expectations and reality. It means we have certain expectations which remain unfulfilled and hence the gap and disappointment. Striving for progress is excellence, whereas striving for perfection is both neurotic and unrealistic. There is no such thing as perfection. There is nothing that cannot be done better the next time.

Here is one example.

- A secretary does a hundred letters perfectly, but in the hundred and first one there is an error. Guess what the boss picks? The error. Should he not pick the error? Can he let the letter go with an error? The answer is absolutely not. But the question is, did the secretary do it on purpose?

How we respond to the gap determines our level of stress.

Unrealistic expectations of perfection from one another can create great stress and break down a relationship.

Your child comes home with a report card. He has five A's and one B. Guess what the parents say. 'Why the B?' You think the kid tried for the B? Does that mean we should accept the B? The answer is no. You never lower your standards. How do you handle it? Acknowledge the A's by saying, 'Great job, you got five A's. Next time we'll see all six.'

Be realistic, not a perfectionist.

'Perfection is not attainable, but if we chase perfection, we can catch excellence.'

– Vince Lombardi

ACTIVITY

1. Identify one major take-home from this chapter.

    _____

    _____

    _____

2. Identify three unrealistic expectations that you have
    from yourself that are causing you stress.

    _____

    _____

    _____

3. How do you plan to overcome these?

    _____

    _____

    _____

4. Identify three unrealistic expectations that you have
    from others that are causing you stress.

    _____

    _____

    _____

5. How do you plan to overcome these?

    _____

    _____

    _____

25

Develop a Support System

There is a correlation between the internal state of one's mind and stressors. Stressors may or may not produce stress, and sometimes we may feel stress without stressors. In other words, there may or may not be a relation between stress and stressors. The good news is that we can deal with stressors without experiencing stress, which means we can learn to deal calmly with hostile situations at home or at work. Restructuring our thought process is a mechanism to cope with change and stress.

- Develop a support group. Emotional support is crucial for dealing with the difficulties of life which cause high stress. Support groups can help you in the following manner:
  - Emotionally supportive friends and relatives who see you as capable can be encouraging and can help address your concerns.
  - It will help you build your self-esteem and a sense of autonomy.
  - Build a network of social relationships which can become a support group. Look at different relationships for different kinds of support.

     To avoid disappointment, always reach out to people you can trust and count on.

– Be proactive. Take initiative and reach out to others instead of waiting for others to reach out to you. Reach out not only to seek help but to extend a helping hand. Join a socially active group to extend your network, for example, a bike-riding group or a book club.

– Don't hesitate to ask for help. You could reach out to senior community groups, local libraries or local branches of national organizations.

• Build a circle of friends or people who are positive and upbeat in life, with good values. We all have our good days and bad days, highs and lows. The support group helps lift you during your lows and you help them in turn. Have frequent get-togethers with such people. These need not be expensive or elaborate. The idea is to spend time together. Being part of a mutual support group is a great way of managing and preventing stress proactively.

Seek professional help if needed. At times stress levels are so high that a person needs professional help. But this carries a stigma, and many people are reluctant to seek professional help.

Don't hesitate to seek help from friends, relatives and professionals. Many times it is our ego that prevents us from seeking help. We also think it is a sign of weakness, not realizing that we are compounding our problems and stress. If you are the kind of person who believes in building relationships, you will be pleasantly surprised at how many people will come forward to help, provided you don't abuse their generosity.

In 1938, Harvard researchers embarked on a decades-long study to find out what makes people happy. What answer do you think they came up with after eighty-five years of research? Career achievement, money, exercise or a healthy diet? No, it is positive relationships. The most consistent finding through eighty-five years of study was that positive relationships keep us happier and healthier and help us live longer.[13]

ACTIVITY

1. Identify one major take-home from this chapter.

    _____

    _____

    _____

2. Identify an area in your life where you feel you need
    support.

    _____

    _____

    _____

3. I commit to finding a support group or a professional
    who can help me with this area of my life.

26

Accept Responsibility

We must accept responsibility and stop blaming others.

Acceptance of responsibility is a sign of maturity. By accepting responsibility, we take control of our lives and show that we are in charge.

John, who was in tenth grade, was always busy playing video games on his computer. In the process, he neglected his chores at home. His parents were concerned about his careless behavior. They wanted to teach him a lesson on responsibility and accountability. They asked John to take care of their dog, Buddy. John agreed to do it but got back to his old ways and neglected Buddy. He neither took him on walks nor fed him, and Buddy fell sick. Seeing this, the concerned parents asked John, 'How would you like it if we treated you the way you treated Buddy? What if we skipped a couple of your meals and you fell sick?' John realized his mistake immediately, apologized and committed to making amends in his behavior. He learned the true meaning of responsibility and accountability that day and thereafter practiced it all his life.

Avoid making excuses and accept responsibilities. Stop rationalizing your mistakes or failures. Stop making excuses and blaming others. When we rationalize our failures, we lose the ability to learn from our mistakes. Losers say, 'It wasn't my fault' or 'They told me to', but winners accept responsibility and say, 'I am sorry I made a mistake, but I have learned from this experience' or 'I accept it was my responsibility'.

Don't accuse people. Delegate responsibility only to those people who are willing to accept it. Have you noticed that there are some people who always blame others or make excuses for non-performance? They don't do the right thing the first time, or they are careless. Hence, they have to redo their stuff again. If you observe carefully, there is a pattern and consistency in their negative behavior. This is not a coincidence; it is a lack of acceptance of responsibility.

Responsibility is a learned skill. It is something we accept and do consciously. It comes from pride in performance. Remember to trust only those who are trustworthy. Take responsibility – if you wait for others to do things for you, you will be waiting for too long. Take charge, whether it is paying your bills or any other obligation. People who accept responsibility make commitments, not promises. Some examples of lack of responsibility: not showing up, coming late, not keeping the other party informed and not delivering in a timely manner.

As long as we blame outside sources, our miseries will continue, and we will feel helpless. Unless we accept responsibility for our feelings and behavior, we cannot change.

The first step is to ask yourself:

- Why did I get upset?
- Why am I angry?

- Why am I depressed?

The moment we answer these we start getting the clues to overcome them.

Every person has two birthdays in life. First, when he comes into this world, and second, when he accepts his responsibilities.

ACTIVITY

1. Identify one major take-home from this chapter.

   _____

   _____

   _____

2. Identify three irresponsible behaviors in yourself
   that you would like to change.

   _____

   _____

   _____

3. Identify three areas in your life where you
   demonstrate responsibility.

   _____

   _____

   _____

27

Don't Make Everything a Prestige Issue in Life

People with fragile egos make everything a prestige issue. They take everything to heart and feel hurt or insulted at the drop of a hat. Practice humility, and keep your ego in control.

Don't take a refusal or rejection personally. Why do we take things personally? Because we have a fragile ego. We become stressed out, paralyzed and unproductive.

When I was selling life insurance, I learned that life insurance was the toughest thing to sell. I had to make ten presentations to make one sale, which means a 90 percent rejection rate. I got nine rejections to make one sale. Sadly, most people take rejection personally, and they get demotivated and quit. They don't realize that they are not being rejected personally. It may be that the product or the company is being rejected or the buyer is not ready to make a purchase.

Unfortunately today, we are taught only two words: **success** and **win**. We are not taught how to lose and fail, even though failure is a reality for all of us. Life does not always go up, up, up; it also comes down. Since we have not learned how to fail or lose, when failure comes we do not know how to handle it. Hence, people go into deep depression and some others even commit suicide.

People with fragile egos do not pay heed to constructive feedback; they become either defensive or offensive. It is also difficult for them to apologize because it hurts their ego. People with high self-esteem evaluate the feedback. And if it makes sense, they accept and implement it.

Many times people say things to us which we take personally, and we feel offended. People may say unsavory things inadvertently or maliciously, and we feel offended. Whatever the motive, why should we feel bad?

For example, somebody calls me a donkey. I need to ask myself, do I have four legs and two long ears? If not, why should I feel offended?

ACTIVITY

1. Identify one major take-home from this chapter.

     _____

     _____

     _____

2. Identify three incidents where you took things
    personally.

     _____

     _____

     _____

3. How do you plan to overcome them?

     _____

     _____

     _____

28

Is Life Fair?

Accept the fact that life is not always fair. Life is like a roller coaster. It goes both ways, up and down. Don't expect problems in life, but be prepared for them. The greatest boxers or champions fight to win, but they are not afraid to lose. Otherwise they would not fight again. Do not be disappointed when you are let down. It is not unusual that people do not keep to their commitments and behave irresponsibly. People show up late, and many times, they do not show up at all, especially when you need them. That is why it is important to always have a backup plan. If you expect the unexpected, you will rarely be disappointed in life. Life isn't fair, but it's still a gift. What you make of it is up to you.

Life is not fair, and it never will be. Get over it.

ACTIVITY

1. Identify one major take-home from this chapter.

   _____

   _____

   _____

2. Identify three times in your life where you let down others.

   _____

   _____

   _____

3. How do you react when you are the one being let down? What can you do better?

   _____

   _____

   _____

29

Don't Become a Pressure Cooker

We must learn to unwind, learn to relax. What comes first, a relaxed mind or a relaxed body? Well, who cares. What came first, the chicken or the egg? Who cares. Either way, we end up with omelets. The same thing applies to our mind and body. It may not be worth our time to analyze this, but either way, you should end up relaxing. A relaxed mind leads to a relaxed body and vice versa.

Some people believe our thoughts and feelings are more important, while others do physical activities to relax. Either way, they end up relaxing and that's what matters.

Take a proactive not reactive approach. Don't take out your anger or frustration on a third party. Don't bottle up your emotions; you may end up exploding like a bomb. Don't bottle up like a pressure cooker. Learn to release tension by talking to someone who is close to you or is supportive of you. Let me share an example here.

Once a hunter returned home, and he loosened the string on his bow. His wife asked, 'Honey, why did you loosen the string?' The hunter replied, 'Whenever the bow is not in use, I loosen the string, because if I don't, it will lose its power to rebound and will fail me when I go hunting.'

Just the way the bow needs to relax when it is not being used, we all need to unwind when we are not working. Unwinding can be done in a million ways. You could just sit, relax and meditate or you could pick a sport and play. You could go out with friends to let your hair down once in a while. Socializing not only rejuvenates you, it also rids you of anxiety, making you more productive in the following days.

Sometimes disengage. Disengaging is called preventive maintenance. When you feel frustrated, burnt out or irritable, before you get to the boiling point or before you explode, it is better to unplug and take time to cool down and relax.

R + R = R + R
Rest + Relaxation = Recovery + Recharge

If we don't give our body preventive maintenance, it will require repairs and recovery. Any stress that goes unchecked will eventually accumulate and manifest itself as a heart attack, nervous breakdown, aches and pains, gastroenteritis, etc. Negative energy will surface and destroy something within us. We often keep working even when our body is hurting badly. We need to learn to listen to our body – the aches and pains, the stiffness in the neck and shoulder muscles, cramps in the stomach, etc. – and attend to it. Our personal effectiveness depends on our health and energy.

Take a break before you break down. Take time off. Set aside quiet time. Keep ten minutes a day for yourself to reflect and meditate. Yoga has some relaxation techniques. Close your eyes, talk to your body parts to get them to relax. Get in touch with yourself. It takes a little practice. It is simple but effective to bring alignment to the body, mind and spirit.

Relaxation techniques can help overcome almost any kind of discomfort and stress. Labor pains are of great discomfort to a woman, yet millions of women bear labor pains and give birth with little or no medication. They do this by practicing breathing and muscle relaxation techniques. Relaxation exercises definitely relieve pain and discomfort. Eventually they make a person emotionally stable and prevent impaired thinking. That helps prevent small matters spiraling into big ones.

Relaxation is not laziness. It is earned leisure time. Unearned leisure is laziness. The time to relax is the time when you don't have the time for it.

Sometimes the most productive thing one can do is relax.

ACTIVITY

1. Identify one major take-home from this chapter.

    _____

    _____

    _____

2. Create your own personal stress-handling program before you become a pressure cooker.

    _____

    _____

    _____

3. List three methods you plan to use to overcome stress.

    _____

    _____

    _____

30

Conflict Resolution

Avoid conflicts. So long as there are human beings on this planet, conflicts are here to stay.

Conflict resolution is a vital skill; it's a prerequisite for happiness. Luckily, this is a skill that can be learned. I share below a few tips on how to resolve conflicts in our relationships. You need to learn them and then pass them on to your friends, colleagues and family members, because nobody is teaching them these skills. If we learn these skills, life will become peaceful, happy and fulfilled.

Learn to become a peacemaker.

What does that mean? First, let us see what peacemaking is not.

It is neither appeasement nor avoidance, nor is it tolerance. Some people say, 'I keep peace wherever I go; I mind my own business, and I don't rock the boat, so I am at peace.' That is not peacemaking – it is avoidance. Appeasement means I always give in and let the other person have their way. That means the other party always wins. Peacemaking is not about running away from the problem. Appeasement means peace at any price. Peaceful and wise people never run away from conflict. They know how to face it and deal with it.

Do we need to learn how to restore peace? Absolutely. At any given time, there are several conflicts going on in the world. There are conflicts between generations, between sexes, between races, between communities, between religions, between political parties, between the rich and the poor, between the educated and the illiterate.

Interpersonal conflicts are inevitable in every walk of life because of a competitive environment, scarce resources, etc. An unhealthy, competitive environment often leads to aggressive behavior, especially where people are immature. Unfortunately, conflict resolution is not taught at home or at work in a proper, structured manner; hence, we become defensive or offensive. In such situations, one can neither fight nor can one quit. As a result, the continuous stress of the status quo converts into chronic stress.

What is the best way to handle confrontation? The best way is to avoid it. Go around it. Sometimes avoiding confrontation is considered a sign of weakness or cowardice. It may not be so. On the contrary, it could be a smart and good strategy. *In martial arts, they teach you that when someone takes a crack at you, the best thing to do is to step away.* Don't try to confront and fight every challenge in the world.

Choose your battles carefully. Be selective.

Remember, no matter how good a communicator you are, there is no way in this world that you can make everyone think from your point of view. It will never happen. **No matter which side you are on, there are some people in this world who are permanently on the other side.**

This world is full of people with different reasonings, and there are some people who are innocent and some who are ignorant, some egoistic, some arrogant, some stupid and some just stubborn. Trying to convert everybody to your way of thinking may be very stressful and a waste of time.

If you are not on the same wavelength as everyone you meet, it is OK. There are times when the chemistry is not right.

If you find yourself in a conflict, disengage. Remember, people under stress generally become unreasonable. You can deal with them as follows:

- Let them blow off steam or let them vent completely
- Do not interrupt
- Listen to them very carefully – both to the surface issues and the underlying issues
- Empathize – give feedback of what you have understood of their problems. Show empathy.
- Restate the problem the way you have understood it
- Handle the person before you handle the problem.
- Stay solution-focused
- Highlight a point of agreement or start your conversation with one

Peace is not the absence of conflicts but the ability to handle conflict in a befitting manner.

The golden rule for conflict resolution: treat others the way you would like to be treated.

ACTIVITY

1. Identify one major take-home from this chapter.

   _____

   _____

   _____

2. Recall a situation from your life that has led to conflict. How could it have been avoided?

   _____

   _____

   _____

3. Identify three ways in which you can improve your conflict management skills.

   _____

   _____

   _____

4. I commit to making the following change:

   _____

   _____

   _____

31

Seek Help

We must not fight our battles alone. Seek help. Learn to use all your strength. But don't try to fight all your battles alone.

Once a young boy told his father, 'I am going to the park to remove the large rock from the middle of the park. It is obstructing things.' After two hours, the boy came back. The father asked, 'Were you able to move the rock?' The son said, 'No, but I am going back again tomorrow.' The same thing happened the next day and the son said, 'I will go back again tomorrow.' The third day, the father quietly followed his son without the son knowing it. He saw his son pushing the rock with all his might, sweating all over. He was out of breath. The father, who was calm and composed, asked his son, 'Are you using all your strength?' The son kept pushing hard and said, 'Yes, Dad, I am using all my strength.' The father said, 'Son, you never asked me. Am I not part of your strength?'

What a powerful message!

We must learn to use all our strengths.

Often, we keep fighting all our battles alone, and we bring stress to our lives. Why do we hesitate to seek help? Are we not part of the strength of our families, teams, etc. when they need our help or support? Should we or will we not stand by them?

Yes, we need to do our own stuff, and we need to teach those close to us to be independent and to do things on their own. But keep in mind that our lives are connected to one another and no one is stronger than us together. **Learn to live by the word 'we' not 'me'.**

The sum total is greater than its parts. That's what togetherness is all about.

ACTIVITY

1. Identify one major take-home from this chapter.

    _____

    _____

    _____

2. Identify three avenues of help that you can use to avoid/overcome stress.

    _____

    _____

    _____

Problems are a part of living. But finding solutions is the art of living.

32

Convert Problems to Solutions

Become solution-focused not problem-focused. The personality trait of some people is such that they look for problems – and they find enough. They have a problem for every solution. They are pessimistic. Positive thinkers are not stupid, and they realize there are problems. Become an optimistic person. Being optimistic does not mean you ignore facts – it means you are focused on solutions.

As a nation the Japanese have always enjoyed eating fresh seafood. However, as time went by the coastal fish population declined, forcing fishermen to go deeper into the ocean to obtain the catch. To accomplish this, the Japanese fishing vessels had to be made bigger. The farther the fishermen went, the more time it took them to bring the fish back to the market. Since the journey took longer, the fish started losing freshness, and the customers were dissatisfied. To address this concern, the fishermen started using freezers in their vessels. This helped them to travel farther and stay longer at sea, which resulted in greater supply. Yet the Japanese customers could clearly differentiate between the frozen and the fresh fish, and the fish became undesirable again. As a solution, the fishing companies installed a tank in their ships and kept the fish alive by putting them into the tanks. Unfortunately, the Japanese people still did not enjoy the taste as the fish in the tank did not move about and lost their fresh taste. What was the final solution that the Japanese created? The Japanese fishing companies still bring fish in the big tank, but now they put a small shark in the tank. The shark does eat a few fish, but it keeps all the others kicking and running. This has resulted in a booming business for the fishermen again.

'If I had an hour to solve a problem, I'd spend fifty-five minutes thinking about the problem and five minutes thinking about the solutions.'
– Albert Einstein

ACTIVITY

1. Identify one major take-home from this chapter.

    _____

    _____

    _____

2. Identify three problems you need to find creative
    solutions for.

    _____

    _____

    _____

3. How do you plan to implement these solutions?

    _____

    _____

    _____

Build a nest egg.
Money in your bank
is more precious
than designer
clothes in your
closet.

33

Live Within Your Means

Overcome financial stress. Live within your means.
Spending more than you earn is a recipe for disaster.
Get on a budget and a systematic savings program.

- If your outflow is more than your inflow, you are heading for trouble
- Whenever you want to buy something, ask yourself if you really need it; if you don't, then don't buy it. That is the only way to become financially strong
- Get on a systematic savings and investment program. Systematic savings has the power of compounding
- Upskill yourself to increase your earnings
- Don't try to keep up with the Joneses
- Don't put on a mask in order to create a false image
- Don't buy things just because they are on sale

Buying things on sale can drain your wealth. When people see sales, such as two for one or buy one get one free, they jump at it and think they are getting something for nothing. Advertisements entice you to buy now or lose forever, and many people live by this misconception that by spending more you save more.

This philosophy has driven many people and even some nations into bankruptcy. Remember, cash is king.

Whenever you want to do an impulse buy, wait for a few days; if you still need it badly, then go buy it. Give yourself a cooling period. **Let your mind be the guide, not your impulses or emotions.**

There are some people who buy things that they don't need, with the money they don't have, to impress people to whom they don't mean a thing.

Conserve your resources. Wastage of anything, whether it is time or money, can be stressful. It erodes your assets, creates resentment and leads to ill health. Build and conserve your resources. Resources such as health, finance and relationships are crucial. They act as an insurance policy during bad times.

Money is not everything, but it certainly helps overcome the pain with comfort.

Don't Be Misguided by Fads and Advertisements

Today, public opinion is being formed by companies that spend billions of dollars to sell their products. They hire the best models and talent. They define beauty and good looks, and if you do not buy their product, you feel inadequate and guilty. Good advertisements make you feel that by using their product, you will look as attractive as the model. Don't let the media add stress to your life.

Don't become a victim of gimmicks. It will cost you heavily both financially and emotionally. Don't be gullible. Living by fads is a recipe for disaster and an invitation to stress.

Make simplicity a way of life. Don't complicate your life with superficial issues.

Remember, a pleasant demeanor makes you look more attractive than being loaded with all the jewelry in the world. **You don't have to spend a million to look like a million.**

Remember, substance is more important than form.

Don't Put on a False Mask

Those who try to keep up with the Joneses approach gift giving and receiving based on other people's opinions. If someone who is financially independent gives them an expensive gift, they will try to match it. A person who is living their life based on other people's standards will try to match their gifts, not realizing what they can afford and what they cannot. A gift is an emotional appreciation and not a display of financial wealth, unless the purpose of the gift is to help the other person financially. That changes the motive from gift giving to extending a helping hand or being empathetic.

Remember, luxury and lies have a high maintenance cost, but simplicity and truth are easy to maintain.

ACTIVITY

1. Identify one major take-home from this chapter.

   _____

   _____

   _____

2. Identify three areas where you are spending money impulsively and causing yourself stress.

   _____

   _____

   _____

3. What will you do to change it?

   _____

   _____

   _____

There is no better pillow than a clear conscience.

34

Integrity Always

We must be truthful and practice integrity.

Integrity is doing the right thing even when the stakes are high and no one is watching.

While returning home from work, John found a wallet on the footpath containing a large amount of cash and ID cards. John was tempted to keep the money, but his conscience bothered him, and he decided to turn in the wallet at the police station. The rightful owner, an elderly lady, was called and the wallet was handed over to her. She was very thankful to John as this was her emergency fund for a rainy day. She offered John a cash reward, which he graciously refused to accept. He said, 'I returned the wallet not with any expectation of a reward but because this was the right thing to do. I would expect the same behavior from anyone else if I lost my wallet.'

***

Sarah paid for the merchandise she had bought from a store with a large-denomination note and received change in return. While sitting in her car, she counted the change and found that she had received an excess amount from the cashier. She went back to the store and returned the excess amount, explaining the discrepancy. The grateful cashier thanked Sarah sincerely and said that such mistakes could cost her her job.

In these two examples the amount at stake was not important. What was important was doing the right thing even when nobody was watching or doing the right thing, even when you know you will not get caught.

What is the moral of the two stories?

Integrity is not absence of temptations but overcoming temptations.

Honesty and integrity are the greatest tranquilizers. Being truthful and practicing integrity brings tremendous peace of mind and is a great stress buster. People who are truthful don't have to remember what they said earlier. Hence, their mind is at peace. **Honest behavior is the foundation of peace of mind and bliss.** The more honest a person is in life, the less stressed he is. Why? Because whenever a person lies, steals or cheats, there is always a fear of getting caught, and hence, he is uneasy and stressed. He falls in his own eyes, develops an inferiority complex and remains stressed.

Dishonesty and lies are big stress creators.

- They lower your self-esteem.
- Often, people tell white lies considering they are small lies. They don't realize that their small lies accumulate and make them a habitual liar.

It's like having a sword hanging over your head. We all carry our own heaven and hell in our minds, and we don't need to die to experience these.

Integrity means authenticity, and it starts with the self. If we cannot be honest with ourselves, who can we be honest with? Authenticity means being sincere, which in turn means saying what you mean and meaning what you say. Keep your conduct above board – your conduct is a reflection of your character. This is what earns you respect and credibility.

Values

Whenever we go against our value system, our self-esteem goes down and stress goes up. Whenever we do something wrong, like lying, stealing and cheating, even if no one is watching, we fall in our own eyes. Whenever we do something positive in life, even if no one is watching, we rise a little bit in our own eyes. That is the magic of self-esteem.

Let your values guide your decisions. A clear statement of purpose gives direction to life. People who lack clarity cannot make wise choices. The biggest cause of our stress is when we go against our values.

Integrity can only be tested against temptation. Till then it is only speculation.

ACTIVITY

1. Identify one major take-home from this chapter.

   _____

   _____

   _____

2. Identify three areas where you can practice integrity at work.

   _____

   _____

   _____

3. Identify three areas where you can practice integrity at home.

   _____

   _____

   _____

4. I commit to leading a life of integrity.

35

Always Positive for the Good

Look for the positive. Learn to be positive.

There is an ancient tale about a king who had a close friend who was always looking at the positives in things. Whenever anything happened, he would say that it was for the good. One day, the king accidentally severed his thumb, and the friend as usual said that it was good. The king was mighty displeased and sent his friend to jail. A few months later, the king went out hunting and got lost. In the deep forest, some tribespeople captured him and wanted to offer him as a sacrifice to their gods. As the priest was tying his hands, he noticed that the king's thumb was missing. Being superstitious, he felt this would be an incomplete sacrifice and would invite divine rage. Hence, he set the king free. When the king came back, he remembered his friend's remark when he had lost his thumb, and he felt great remorse. He went to his friend and apologized. The king said to his friend, 'You were right. It was because I lost my thumb in the accident that I am alive today; but wasn't it bad that I sent you to jail?' The friend said, 'No, it was good.' The king wanted to know what was good about it. His friend replied, 'If you had not sent me to jail, I would have accompanied you on the hunting trip, and I would have been sacrificed instead.'

If you analyze the above story, the objective is to be optimistic, not fatalistic. Look for the positive. Being positive does not mean that a person has to jump up and down like a monkey or agree with everyone on everything. Being positive means that a person is aware of the challenges in life, but they are solution-focused. They focus more on what can be done rather than on what cannot be done. They think of possibilities.

With positive thinking we can do everything much better than with negative thinking. There is a misconception that we can do everything with positive thinking. That's not true. No matter how positive I am, I cannot do a bypass surgery on someone and have them live; they'd die under my knife.

Positive thinking does not guarantee success. Positive thinking with positive efforts and actions increases our probability of success.

ACTIVITY

1. Identify one major take-home from this chapter.

    _____

    _____

    _____

2. Identify three areas of your life where you can convert fatalistic behavior into positive behavior.

    _____

    _____

    _____

36

No Toxicity

Stay away from toxins and toxic people. Timeless wisdom says that we should choose companions who uplift us and be someone who uplifts others. As the old saying goes, you are the average of five individuals you spend most of your time with. It emphasizes the importance of surrounding yourself with people who bring out the best in you. We need to devise strategies on how to navigate through challenging relationships. **Toxic people have a magical ability to suck positivity out of any situation, eventually leaving you drained.**

Toxic people are infectious and carriers of stress. These negative people are habitual moaners, groaners and complainers. They are pessimistic. If you take them to the land of milk and honey, the only thing they will see are calories and cholesterol. In fact, they are carriers of darkness and bring brightness when they leave. Stay away from them unless you are stuck with them, for example, if they are your relatives. Don't encourage them in any manner. Stay away from negative, selfish, rude, dishonest, insincere people. Learn to cut your losses in life.

Choose your friends carefully. If you want to reduce stress, surround yourself with positive people who make you feel good about yourself. When you see good and feel good, you attract more good. There is an old saying that if you lie down with dogs, you will wake up with fleas. **Your friends and peer group reflect your choices and personality. Choose wisely.**

Be a pleasant person. Being pleasant helps you improve the quality of relationships. Stay away from toxic people and don't become a toxic person yourself.

You will have noticed some people are pleasant and warm human beings. They bring a relaxed aura wherever they go. A pleasant person is warm, polite, courteous and always welcome. Learn to be pleasant. Practice being pleasant, and soon it will become a way of life. It relieves stress, relaxes people, promotes cooperation, develops friendship and builds relationships. It relieves stress not only for one's self but for whoever one meets.

Treat others with respect and dignity. Some people are courteous or pleasant only when they have something to gain from others. They use courtesy and pleasantness as a strategy. When we use them as a strategy, it is crooked. Positive people make pleasantness a way of life. Put on a genuine smile.

To some people unpleasantness comes naturally, while to some pleasantness comes naturally.

We should be grateful to toxic people as they show us what we should not be.

Ask yourself what kind of person you are to others. Are you uplifting them by adding value to their life or draining their energies by making it worse?

You cannot have a positive life with a negative mindset.

Don't feed negativity. Thoughts have a multiplier effect. One positive or negative thought multiplies into a hundred more, and it becomes a chain. One negative thought can lead to frustration, disheartenment and disgust. The way out is to get involved in constructive and productive activities. Give yourself a time limit, for example, that you will not let a negative thought continue beyond ten minutes.

Allowing negative thoughts to persist is like inviting a thief into your house to steal your peace of mind.

We must stay away from negative influences.

What are negative influences? Negative influences are negative people, drugs, alcohol, pornography and profanity. They pull people down. They destroy lives. They destroy families. They destroy the peace in society. They only bring stress. It is better to stay away from them than to get in and later try to get out. Remember, prevention is better than cure.

Positivity energizes. Negativity drains.

<u>Activity</u>

1. Identify one major take-home from this chapter.

   _____

   _____

   _____

2. Identify three toxic behaviors that are pulling you down.

   _____

   _____

   _____

3. I commit to making the following change in my life:

   _____

   _____

   _____

37

Comparison: A Recipe for Disaster

Stop making comparisons. Constantly seeking what someone else has is a recipe for dissatisfaction and disaster. The expectations we place on ourselves based on those we are comparing ourselves with may not be a fair comparison to begin with. We don't know their background, upbringing, circumstances, etc. Such comparisons are more likely to diminish our self-worth and cause resentment. If we find others more competent, we feel insecure and start distrusting our own abilities. Constantly measuring ourselves against others can create a cycle of negativity and self-criticism. It can lead to feelings of jealousy and low self-esteem.

Some people put too much emphasis on material things. They keep looking at the kind of clothes you wear, the kind of jewelry you have, the kind of car you drive, the kind of home you live in. Why? Because they judge your worth by your net worth. Not only do they judge your worth by your net worth but they also judge their own self-worth by their net worth. No wonder they have a hard time keeping up with the Joneses.

Experience shows that keeping up with the Joneses causes both financial and emotional distress. What does keeping up with the Joneses mean? It means always comparing yourself with others and wanting what they have, whether you can afford it or not.

Such people are very shallow. They don't understand that people make things, things don't make people.

Most of your friends want to see you do well in life but not better than them.

It is not unusual to see a neighbor who has won a jackpot buy a boat. Not wanting to be left behind, the other neighbors begin to think they need one too, even though they cannot afford it. It is nice to enjoy some luxury as long as it fits in your budget but not when you buy stuff and go neck-deep into debt just to impress your neighbor. The reality is that you don't own the stuff, the stuff owns you. The debt takes over, steals your income, and suddenly you become a slave to the things you thought would brighten up your life.

Steps to stop making comparisons:

- Practice gratitude. Be grateful for what you have and where you are.
- Learn the power of contentment. Permanent discontentment creates multiple problems.
  Gratitude leads to contentment. Contentment does not mean that you don't have ambitions and goals. It means being at peace with yourself and planning for a better future.
- Reduce social media usage; it doesn't always reflect reality. It does not give the complete picture of other people's lives. It only gives the highlights: reels.
- Focus on your strengths, be humble, but be proud of your strengths. Don't put yourself down; don't

degrade yourself. The more we compare ourselves with others, the worse we feel about ourselves.

- Start celebrating other people's successes no matter how big or small they are. Cheer others. When a friend tells you about her promotion or about buying a new home, be happy and enthusiastic and keep the focus on them. **Just because others are winning does not mean you are losing.** Their success has nothing to do with you.
- Learn to compete with yourself.

Good rules to follow:

- Set a time limit of no more than thirty minutes to scroll social media. Step away after thirty minutes.
- Turn off your phone when having dinner with family and friends. Why? To stay focused. Give respect to the people around you.
- Don't feel obligated to reply to every comment. Nobody has the time or obligation to do that.
- Lastly, spend time and energy on your blessings, such as your family, friends, home, job. There are others who may be jealous of you. There may be plenty of people comparing themselves with you and desiring everything you have.

Keep competition constructive. Don't strive to be faster, richer or smarter than others. **Positive people are like athletes who compete against themselves. They better their own records.**

A human life is a work in progress; it is a process of continuous improvement.

Our objective is progress, not perfection.

ACTIVITY

1. Identify one major take-home from this chapter.

   _____

   _____

   _____

2. Write down three things about yourself that you are really proud of.

   _____

   _____

   _____

3. When something good happens to others, what is your natural reaction. Are you happy or jealous? Reflect on your reactions. If jealous, you are a victim of the comparison trap.

4. Take a holiday from social media. Start with a day and slowly build up to a week without social media.

5. Recall a time when you compared yourself with someone and found yourself lacking.

6. Is there a way to look at the above situation in a more positive light?

   _____

   _____

   _____

7. I commit to making the following change:

   _____

   _____

   _____

38

We Must Get Organized

Being organized shows clarity of thinking. It makes it easy to plan life and access information.

Quoting the stats database of the National Association of Professional Organizers, Huffpost.com says, **'30 percent of all employees' time is spent trying to find lost documents'.**[14]

Being disorganized and not planning properly leads to chaos. Chaos leads to confusion and confusion leads back to chaos. Chaos wastes time and causes stress. It becomes a cycle. It shows lack of clarity in thinking. Hence, we perform random activities without prioritizing. Random activity leads to activity without accomplishment and drains energy, leading to fatigue and stress.

Maintain order to easily retrieve things such as important papers, pens, pencils and spectacles. It will save your time and relieve stress.

Prepare for the next day the night before.

When I was selling life insurance in the U.S., it was common practice to make sale appointments a week in advance. What I learned was that if you don't have appointments made one week in advance and if you wake up in the morning and start thinking 'what do I do today', you are unemployed with a job. Sadly, I find most people in sales don't have appointments made a week in advance.

Not planning in advance brings chaos and in turn leads to stress. We can be relaxed and sleep well when we know that we are prepared for the next day.

Organizing is not about perfection; it's about efficiency, reducing clutter, saving time and improving your overall quality of life.

Declutter your home and workplace regularly at least once a month. Get organized but not regimented to the point of rigidity. That would be counterproductive.

With organization comes empowerment.

Organize yourself before you organize anything else.

ACTIVITY

1. Identify one major take-home from this chapter.

    _____

    _____

    _____

2. Identify three areas at work where you can get organized and relieve stress.

    _____

    _____

    _____

3. Identify three areas at home where you can get organized and relieve stress.

    _____

    _____

    _____

We need to distinguish between LITTLE and CRUCIAL versus PETTY and TRIVIAL.
Don't be petty and short-sighted.

39

Little and Crucial Versus Petty and Trivial

Little and Crucial

I know a billionaire who owns many properties. As he was walking through one of his factory premises, he saw some scrap papers on the floor. He stopped to pick them up. He didn't call anyone to ask them to pick up the papers. He just did it himself. Analyze his behavior. What message did his staff get? They saw leadership by example. Small details do matter. It inspired everyone to pay attention to the smallest details.

Have you ever been bitten by an elephant? Probably not. Have you ever been bitten by a mosquito? The answer is that all of us have been, many times. **It is the little, little things that make the big difference. But if they make such a big difference, how can they be little?** What a paradox!

'Don't major in minor things' does not mean ignoring the little that is important but distinguishing between little and crucial and petty and trivial.

Remember, all little things are not little.

- An army of soldiers with the best arms cannot fight and win the battle if they have no shoes.
- It is the small leak that sinks the ship.
- It is the small spark of fire that destroys the forest.

Once, one of the computers at our office didn't have a functional UPS, and we asked the concerned person to fix it. Instead of rectifying the problem, he plugged the computer directly into the socket without bothering to fix the UPS. He shrugged off the responsibility by saying, 'It's not a big issue. It's just a little thing.' The question is, when does it become a big issue? When the computer blows up because of a voltage fluctuation, or when we lose important data? Do accidents inform you in advance before they happen? And if an accident does happen, just imagine the loss.

Is that what we're waiting for? How short-sighted and irresponsible! What a callous attitude! In the above example if an accident took place, would you call it an accident? Or was it gross negligence? Was it avoidable? Such negligence is only inviting trouble.

A few questions arise here:

- If the loss happens, who is responsible for it?
- Who compensates for the financial and productivity loss?
- Would just an apology in a careless situation like this be acceptable?

That person in the office looked at the issue as 'petty and trivial' and not 'little and crucial'.

These situations evidently happen in many offices – ignoring small, little things that are crucial is sheer negligence and can be disastrous.

It is much easier to do the right thing the first time, and every time, than to explain why we did not and repent later.

Petty and Trivial

Some people major in minor issues. We need to learn what to attend to, what to look for and what to overlook. We should avoid letting little, little things bother us to the point of becoming unmanageable. Once in a while you find people who behave irresponsibly. They do not show up on time, and they do not have the courtesy to inform you. We respond to them or to such situations with frustration, anger or outrage, because we become emotionally disturbed. This is because we become reactive not proactive.

Many times little, unpleasant surprises happen. Do not let them throw you off and bring stress. Don't let little inconveniences such as minor delays, setbacks and disruptions bother you. Little glitches will always happen in life. If you give them more importance than they deserve, they will only heighten your stress and shorten your life.

Learn to distinguish between a problem and an inconvenience. When we learn to distinguish between a problem and an inconvenience, we learn to distinguish between little and crucial and petty and trivial.

Once in a while just let go. Dogs bark, but the caravan goes on.

Keep little things in perspective. Let small things be small. Don't try to kill butterflies with guns.

ACTIVITY

1. Identify one major take-home from this chapter.

    _____

    _____

    _____

2. Recall an incident when you were unable to distinguish between little and crucial and petty and trivial. What was the outcome?

    _____

    _____

    _____

3. What little things are you ignoring that are causing a negative compounding effect for you?

    _____

    _____

    _____

4. I commit to the following change:

    _____

    _____

    _____

If you have not planned for the unplanned, then you have not planned.

40

Plan for the Unplanned

*A good leader always has Plan A, Plan B, Plan C, Plan D.
Why? Is he planning to fail? The answer is no. He is making
sure that he succeeds no matter what. In the army this is how
a good general plans.*

*In fact, a far-sighted person traveling in a car will make
sure they have a spare tire, a first-aid kit, jumper cables, fire
extinguishers, etc. Many people carry these things when they
are going for a picnic. Of course, we cannot plan for every
contingency in life, but some things are like life jackets – if
you do not have them, you will never need them again.*

**If you have not planned for the unplanned, then
you have not planned.** Leave yourself time in between
tasks for contingencies. Unexpected things do happen.

Experience shows that every properly planned
minute saves you ten in execution.

Another example of insufficient planning is when a
person's cell phone dies because he has not charged it
properly. Not doing things routinely in a proper manner
creates emergencies and disasters that are avoidable.
This is inviting unnecessary stress.

Plan but don't overplan. Have you noticed that there
are some people who go for a vacation with twenty-five

items on the checklist to cover every eventuality. To do this, they keep asking what if, what if, what if questions of themselves.

A good plan well executed is better than a great plan poorly executed.

ACTIVITY

1. Identify one major take-home from this chapter.

   _____

   _____

   _____

2. Identify three areas where proper planning would have prevented problems in your life.

   _____

   _____

   _____

3. How do you plan to overcome them?

   _____

   _____

   _____

41

Become Health-Conscious

Once a doctor told me, 'If you practice four things in life, most of your health problems will disappear.'

1. Maintain a happy demeanor and laugh often
2. Get adequate sleep and rest
3. Follow a healthy diet
4. Build strong relationships for emotional health

If these four practices are missing, you can take all the medicines in the world and still remain sick.

Good health impacts our decision-making process. When we are not in good health, we end up taking decisions that we would not have if we were in good health. *If you bought a million-dollar racehorse, would you feed it junk food, make it drink alcohol, smoke cigarettes and let it sleep all day long or would you feed it a healthy diet and make it exercise daily to keep it fit? If we would give special treatment to the racehorse, then why do we ill-treat our million-dollar bodies? People often make their health the last priority, not realizing that an unhealthy body can never house a healthy and stable mind.*

We must maintain physical fitness. We should follow a regular exercise program at least three to four times a week. If we don't have the time to look after our health today, how will we get the time tomorrow to fall sick? We ruin our health in the pursuit of making money, but when we lose our health, all the wealth in the world cannot bring it back. We need to get our priorities right.

Have you noticed that when we keep a pet, such as a dog, we make sure that the dog eats good food and walks regularly, maybe even three times a day. Why don't we make sure that we too exercise to remain in good health?

How do irrational people justify stupidity? A person once said, 'If I am in good health, I don't need exercise; and if I am not in good health, I can't exercise.' Either way, exercise is not part of his lifestyle.

What a combination of ignorance and stupidity!

When stupidity meets ignorance it is a recipe for disaster.

ACTIVITY

1. Identify one major take-home from this chapter.

   _____

   _____

   _____

2. Identify three activities you plan to start on to gain
   good health.

   _____

   _____

   _____

42

Laughter Is a Medicine

Develop a sense of humor. Our physical condition is deeply connected to our thought process. A healthy mind will attract a healthy body, and a sickly mind will attract a sickly body. A calm mind and good thoughts trigger a chemical reaction in our body that builds our immune system and keeps us in good health. A young person can start looking aged and much older than his actual age by harboring negative thoughts of worry, anger, hate and jealousy. The reverse is just as true.

Dr. Norman Cousins, author of Anatomy of an Illness, *is a prime example of how a person can cure himself of a terminal illness. He had a 1 in 500 chance of recovery, but Dr. Cousins wanted to prove that if there was anything like mind over matter, he'd make it a reality. He figured if negative emotions caused negative chemicals in our body, then the reverse must be true too. Positive emotions, like happiness and laughter, would bring positive chemicals into our system. He moved from the hospital to a hotel and rented humorous movies and literally cured himself by laughing. Of course, medical help is important, but the will to live for the patient is equally, if not more, important. A funny bone could be a lifesaver. Besides, it makes life's adversities easier to handle.*[15]

Humor helps us tide over the tight spots in life. Without humor life becomes very tough. When we are constantly under stress, our perspective changes. We are unable to enjoy ourselves and miss out on the fun in life. Humor is contagious. It can be a lifesaver.

Laughter is being used as therapy. Some studies show that fifteen minutes of laughter is equivalent to approximately two hours of sleep.

Benefits of Laughter

- It reduces the stress hormone cortisol in the body. By incorporating laughter in our lives, we can promote overall well-being.
- When we laugh, our body releases endorphins, and this hormone starts building our immune system. A robust immune system is essential to fight infection and disease. It acts as a mood enhancer, bringing feelings of happiness and contentment. These feel-good hormones help fight anxiety and depression.
- Laughter therapy is gaining recognition as a powerful tool for maintaining emotional balance and reducing stress. It enhances the feel-good factor. A good way of incorporating laughter into our daily life is to share jokes with friends, watch a comedy show or engage in an active laughter exercise.

It is easier to smile than to frown. It improves face value. Who likes to be around a grouch? No one, unless you are a bigger one! A smile is contagious and is an inexpensive way to improve looks. A smiling face is always welcome.

Life is short. Smile while you still have teeth.

A person who does not smile is like a man who has a million dollars in the bank but no checkbook.

ACTIVITY

1. Identify one major take-home from this chapter.

_____

_____

_____

2. Identify three ways in which you plan to incorporate laughter into your life.

_____

_____

_____

43

Don't Delay Your Happiness

We need to differentiate between pleasure and happiness. Pleasure is temporary; happiness is lasting. Pleasure comes from doing or getting something, whereas happiness is a way of life.

For many people happiness is contingent on something, such as buying a car or a home or getting married or having kids. Happiness is an experience which comes from a state of mind, from within; it springs from internal feelings rather than from external events.

Often, it is not the complexities of life that bring unhappiness but the simplicities that we overlook. Happiness is the ultimate goal for everyone. I have never heard of anyone who doesn't want to be happy. Is there a prescription to being happy?

Happiness is a feeling. It is our emotional state of mind. It is our attitude. It is our emotional response to how we see life. We don't appreciate happiness till it starts dwindling away and unhappiness starts seeping in. When we start passing through the tight spots in life, it becomes challenging to stay happy.

To achieve happiness, an important prerequisite is self-acceptance. It leads to high self-esteem, which helps one to be at peace with oneself. It helps build a positive attitude and strong relationships, and it brings emotional balance.

Happiness originates from inside but reflects in behavior outside.

The most unhappy people are those who keep looking for a reason to be happy.

Success and happiness are interconnected in some form or the other with our attitude toward life.

*Almost twenty years ago, I heard a story about a mechanic who once had a very rough day. His tools broke at work. He had a flat tire, then had a minor accident with a truck and then his car stalled on the road. As his colleague drove him home, he was steaming in silence. Upon reaching home, he invited his colleague inside to meet his family. As they were walking towards the door, the mechanic stopped briefly near a flowering bush and touched its tips. Soon after this, as he entered his home, there was a transformation. His face started glowing with warmth and happiness. He had a great smile on his face, hugs and kisses for his children and a warm embrace for his wife. Shortly thereafter, the mechanic went to see off his colleague to the car. As they passed the bush, the colleague asked the mechanic, 'What happened when you touched the bush? You changed completely. How come?' The mechanic replied, 'I have learned an important lesson in my life: **troubles are inevitable but suffering is optional**. I have resolved that whenever I enter my home I shall always stop near that flowering bush and dump all my troubles and problems on it.' Then with a smile he said, 'Every morning when I leave home and I go to the bush to pick up my troubles* *and problems, interestingly, most of them are not there anymore.'*

What a way to live life! What an attitude! This mechanic is probably more qualified than most academics who teach us how to live. He starts his day with happiness and, in spite of everything that happens, ends his day with happiness. That is the key to good relationships.

Drivers of Happiness

- A happy family life
- Strong social bonding between families and friends
- Living a purposeful life
- Maintaining good health
- A positive attitude

Happiness is an inside job, and sometimes you have to create your own sunshine.

ACTIVITY

1. Identify one major take-home from this chapter.

   _____

   _____

   _____

2. Identify three ways in which you plan to bring happiness in your life.

   _____

   _____

   _____

44

Do Your Due Diligence

Problems crop up no matter what, but if a person is not careful in doing their homework, they will be buried under problems, leading to stress and regret.

It is always a good idea to check the depth of the water before jumping in. Before you play a game, clarify the following: (1) The rules of the game. (2) What is the stopping time? (3) What are the stakes?

Before taking a decision, evaluate all consequences, consider the options and ask tough questions. If you commit yourself to a course of action after due diligence, you will save yourself a lot of headache and heartache. Whenever good organizations are purchasing something, they invariably shop around and get a few bids. They also check references. Analyzing them is a great learning experience and a good way to avoid pitfalls. It does not guarantee success, but the odds are in your favor. Your chances of making a wise decision are much higher, and you will have avoided stress.

Test before you trust. These days, it is not uncommon to see even those whom you trusted most turning against you for personal gain. In today's day and age, where values have fallen and morals are shaky, testing the water is very important – be it at work or elsewhere. Blind trust is in fact fatal. It is a good idea to keep personal things personal till one is sure of the other person's trustworthiness.

If you trust someone implicitly, you will either gain a friend for life or a lesson for life. Most of the time it is a lesson for life.

Don't be gullible. Don't be easily drawn in by the positive action of others. Be wise to judge whether or not the action is genuine.

Get your facts right. Reserve your judgments till you have all the facts in hand. Jumping to conclusions without knowing the facts can be disastrous and painful for you and others. Get facts from all sides before coming to any conclusions or decisions. A judge always hears both sides before giving a judgment.

Don't jump to conclusions without knowing the facts.

Activity

1. Identify one major take-home from this chapter.

    _____

    _____

    _____

2. Identify an area in your life where you came under
    stress because you had not done due diligence.

    _____

    _____

    _____

3. Going forward, what would you do to ensure due
    diligence?

    _____

    _____

    _____

Working hard is good but burning out is not good.

45

Working Hard Is Good, Burning Out Is Not

When my elder daughter finished her MBA and got a job with a major consulting firm in the U.S., she was all excited. It was 1999, and there was low unemployment in the U.S. Young kids fresh out of college were getting all kinds of monies, which was unheard of before. This lady in her mid-twenties was consulting with very senior executives of large multinational corporations, flying from one destination to another. Her enthusiasm was high. She used to come home only on the weekends, get her laundry done and by five o'clock on Monday morning she was up to go to the airport again. There was hardly any time for her to relax or unwind. Initially, when she started working, and especially because it was her first job, I asked her, 'How are things?' She said, 'Dad, they're great. It couldn't be better. I'm excited and enjoying it.' This was her introduction to the corporate world. We would touch base only on weekends as she didn't have time otherwise. Every week I used to ask her the same question, 'How are things?' And she would say, 'Dad, they're great. It couldn't be better. I'm excited and enjoying it.' A few months went by, and every time I asked her how things were *there was tremendous enthusiasm in her voice. Gradually, the enthusiasm in her voice dipped and 'It's exciting' turned into 'It's good'. It went on for a few more weeks like this till one day when I asked her, 'How are things?' she said, 'It's OK. No big deal.' Time went by. I knew something was not right, but I didn't probe. And then one day, she broke down when I asked her the same question. She said, 'Dad, it's too much. I am not even able to get the time to breathe.' I told her to sit down and listen carefully. I said, 'Honey, all of us have worked hard in life, and we must work hard because nothing happens without hard work. But hear this carefully. Working hard is good but burning out is not.' I asked her, 'Are you working hard or burning out?' She said, 'Dad, I'm burning out.'*

We have to work hard, and there are times when we put in eighteen hours a day, but if it starts happening day in and day out on an ongoing basis, it starts taking a toll on our health. That is not working hard; that is called burning out. There is certainly something good and noble about working hard, but losing sleep, missing meals and exercise because of excessive work is burning out. Ruining your health physically and mentally can be disastrous and is short-sighted.

One can achieve more by staying fit and healthy and enjoy success in the long haul.

I came across a similar incident many years ago when we were about to hire a person in our office. I mentioned to him that in this job you often had to work late and on weekends. The man's reply was amazing. He taught me a good lesson. He said, 'I am willing to work late, I have no problem in working late, but I have a problem in sitting late.' I said, 'I am confused. Can you explain what you mean and what is the difference.' He said, 'Sir, many offices have a culture where if the boss for some reason is sitting late, and whether there is work or not, he wants his entire team to be in the office till he leaves. If there is work, I have no problem; I am willing to work till midnight. But if there is no work, I would request that you please let me go.' That day I learned the difference between working late and sitting late.

There is a flip side to it. There are many people who do not work during working hours. They actually waste time gossiping and socializing, with the result that they have to sit late to get the job done. They do not realize that this is counterproductive and adds to stress, besides creating a bad environment. Some others sit late so that they can bill for overtime.

Deloitte research in 2023 found that 77 percent of workers have experienced burnout at their current job and over half have experienced burnout more than once in their careers. The top driver of burnout is a lack of support and recognition from leadership.[16]

The WHO has classified burnout as an occupational phenomenon and recommends that the word 'should not be applied to describe experiences in other areas of life'.[17]

Hard work is okay. Burning out is not okay.

Working late is okay. Sitting late is not okay.

Activity

1. Identify one major take-home from this chapter.

   _____

   _____

   _____

2. Identify three areas of your life that led to burnout. How do you plan to overcome that?

   _____

   _____

   _____

3. I commit to changing the following behavior and practicing it for six weeks:

   _____

   _____

   _____

4. By making that one change, how would you benefit?

   _____

   _____

   _____

46

Respect Time

Time is more precious than money. When we waste time, what are we wasting? Our lives.

If you waste time, time will waste you. Don't waste other people's time, and don't let others waste your time either. We have a policy in our office that nobody is allowed to bring their mobile phones into the conference room. Nobody means nobody, including our CEO. Let me ask you, if you came to our office and I kept my mobile with me and if it kept disturbing (even if I put it on silent), would it be courteous to you? No, it will be considered discourteous and ill-mannered, and I will not be able to give you the due attention that you deserve. Will I not be wasting your time? The answer is yes. Do I have the right to waste your time? The answer is no. By not bringing my mobile with me I commit that I shall not waste your time. But I will not let you waste my time either. So I would request that you also leave your mobile outside at the reception.

Practice Punctuality

People who constantly disrespect time invite disaster and trouble. Habitual latecomers generate stress and expose themselves to avoidable mistakes and accidents. Delaying meetings actually penalizes those who arrive on time.

People who do not respect their own time do not respect other people's time either. Get into the habit of being on time and starting and finishing things on time in order to avoid stress.

Benefits of Time Management

- Boosts confidence
- Improves quality of work
- Increases productivity
- Improves work–life balance
- Reduces stress
- Increases relaxation time
- Opens new opportunities
- Enhances energy
- Helps achieve your goals
- Builds self-discipline

Steps to Manage Time Productively

- Prioritize: do what is important
- Plan: create a time-bound action plan
- Become proactive: preempt both problems and opportunities
- Be productive: measure productivity daily
- Personal growth: enhance spiritual and financial growth

We cannot manage time, we can only manage ourselves. Time management is only a name given to life management.

ACTIVITY

1. Identify one major take-home from this chapter.

   _____

   _____

   _____

2. Identify three behaviors you will change to respect
   your time.

   _____

   _____

   _____

3. Identify three behaviors that you will change to
   respect other people's time.

   _____

   _____

   _____

47

Avoid Arguments

What is the best way to win an argument? The answer is by avoiding it. An argument is one thing you will never win in life. You win, you lose. You lose, you lose. You win an argument, you lose a good customer, a good job, a good friend, a good marriage, etc. Most important of all, the victory is empty. **The more arguments you win, the fewer friends you have.**

Discuss, don't argue. What is the difference?

- Discussion throws light; argument throws heat.
- Discussion is an exchange of knowledge; argument is an exchange of ignorance.
- Discussion tries to prove what is right; argument tries to prove who is right.

Arguments can be very stressful. They arise from inflated egos. Avoid them at all costs.

Once a donkey got into an argument with a tiger, and he said, 'The grass is blue.' The tiger said, 'No, the grass is green.' They kept arguing until finally the donkey said, 'Let's go to the king of the jungle and seek his judgment.' So they went to the lion, and the donkey said to the lion, 'I keep saying the grass is blue, but the tiger insists that the grass is green. Please tell us who is right.' Without any hesitation, the lion gave the judgment in favor of the donkey and said that the grass is blue. The donkey was very happy to hear the judgment in his favor, but as he left the court, he had another thought: the king gave the judgment in my favor, but why didn't he punish the tiger for wasting my time? So he went back and requested the king to punish the tiger. The king readily obligated and now punished the tiger by saying, 'You are not allowed to speak for the next three days. You must remain silent.' Now the donkey was happy that he had got the tiger punished. After the donkey left, the tiger asked the king, 'What kind of a judge are you, giving false judgments. You know the grass is green, I know the grass is green, the world knows the grass is green, then why did you give the judgment in favor of the donkey by saying the grass is blue?' The lion replied, 'You know the grass is green, I know the grass is green, the world knows the grass is green, but why are you arguing with the donkey? You are punished only because you are arguing with the donkey.'

Only a bigger fool argues with a fool.

ACTIVITY

1. Identify one major take-home from this chapter.

   _____

   _____

   _____

2. Identify three instances where getting into an argument resulted in a loss for you.

   _____

   _____

   _____

3. How do you plan to overcome such situations?

   _____

   _____

   _____

48

Avoid Litigation

If you want to lead a relaxed life and sleep well, then avoid litigation. Why?

Litigation not only drains you financially but also drains you emotionally.

The only people who win in any litigation are the lawyers. Everybody else is a loser. Even if we have to take a loss, it is better to avoid litigation than go through the aggravation of going to court. It is very stressful and not worth it.

It is not uncommon to see family disputes related to property or other petty matters dragging on for years, causing stress to both parties and draining their financial resources. The only gainers are the lawyers. In fact a judge who was a friend of mine said to me, 'Shiv, you have a great case and are sure to win.' But then he advised me to settle quickly, even if it meant taking a minor loss.

A good doctor avoids unnecessary medication. A good lawyer always advises against unnecessary litigation. Unscrupulous lawyers misguide into litigation. Whenever we have problems, we start building a case for ourselves mentally. We imagine the courtroom battle being won by us. The less stressful way is to somehow negotiate and come to an amicable agreement. Litigation can take years away from your life, and eventually, no matter who wins, both parties end up losing. Make it the last resort and not the first.

Steps to Avoid Litigation

1. Clarify things in writing in order to avoid misunderstandings
2. Opt for legal advice before signing an agreement
3. Stand by your agreement
4. Consider mediation
5. Be prepared to compromise

An unscrupulous lawyer can steal more with his briefcase than a hundred robbers with guns.

ACTIVITY

1. Identify one major take-home from this chapter.

   _____

   _____

   _____

2. What tools can you employ to avoid litigation?

   _____

   _____

   _____

Stop firefighting
all your life.

49

Learn to Make Mature Decisions

Do not rush into making hasty decisions.

The flip side is, take a stand when you need to take a stand. In life we are penalized not for our actions but our inaction when we should have acted. More lies have been told by remaining silent when we should have spoken. Very often, silence and inaction can cause more pain by creating guilt and resentment.

We all have to make multiple decisions in life, and to make decisions we need to get our facts right. But some people procrastinate taking decisions even if they have their facts right. Keep in mind, indecision is also a decision by default. It paralyzes people and is a recipe for crisis.

Success or failure depends on the decisions you make. What brings maturity to a decision? It is the decision-making process, which means the decision behind the decision. Hence, if the process is right, the chances are that eight out of ten times your decision will be right. Indecision can be both a cause and a consequence of stress.

Following the six steps below will help you make better decisions and you will be able to handle close to 90 percent of your problems.

1. Identify if it is a problem or an inconvenience (you will find most of the inconveniences are not problems and can be handled easily).
2. Write down the problem. Writing crystallizes the real problem. Often, 90 percent of the solution lies in properly identifying the problem.
3. Write down the possible causes of the problem.
4. Write down the possible solutions to the problem.
5. Identify the best solutions.
6. Justify or write down the reason why these are the best solutions.

What brings disparity in compensation within the same company? It is not the number of hours that we put in, it is the maturity of the decision-making ability that brings disparity.

Maturity is not when we start speaking big things, it is when we start understanding small things.

ACTIVITY

1. Identify one major take-home from this chapter.

    _____

    _____

    _____

2. Identify three areas of your life where you plan to
    follow the six steps given in this chapter.

    _____

    _____

    _____

50

Learn to Put Work Before Play

It is true that all work and no play makes Jack a dull boy. The reverse is just as true. Play without work or play before work is very stressful.

When you turn on the TV to watch your favorite player, actor, musician or even the millionaires and billionaires and see their luxurious lifestyles, you get tempted and you want it. You want to be a professional athlete or want to own your own business or become a highly paid professional, doctor or lawyer. Obviously we want to have all these nice things but the question is, are we willing to put in the hard work? **Most importantly, hard work comes first and the rewards come later.** After hard work when you receive the reward, it is gratifying because you have earned it.

Children who finish their homework after school and then go out to play enjoy a lot more than those who do the reverse. Why? Somehow they feel relaxed; otherwise it keeps bothering them. At the back of their mind they know that when they go back they have to complete their homework, and if for any reason it is left undone, they will have to face the consequences. The same thing applies at an office. Adults who finish their work can relax better than those who have loads of work pending.

Experience shows that we enjoy leisure much better after we have done a good day's hard work. Procrastination can be very stressful. How can a person have fun when the mind knows that there are so many important things pending? Not doing things when they ought to be done causes avoidable stress. Neglecting work can be stressful. In a balanced cycle of work and fun, work comes first and fun comes as a reward. Why invite avoidable stress?

ACTIVITY

1. Identify one major take-home from this chapter.

    _____

    _____

    _____

2. Identify three areas where you will practice the
    principles of work.

    _____

    _____

    _____

51

Invest in Relationships

Make relationships a pleasure not a pain. To have a friend you need to be a friend. Our biggest asset in this world is not our bank balance but our relationships. What a person with good relationships can achieve with one phone call may not be achieved with a million dollars. Relationships are our biggest support systems. **The poorest person in the world is the one who has millions of dollars in the bank but has no relationships and is emotionally bankrupt.** Relationships are like plants and trees: they need to be nurtured. Otherwise, they just die. Relationships ought to be a win-win proposition where you build each other up. A good relationship is a great stress buster. It gives us emotional security in life. Let affection bind relationships. One needs to spark affection and discard ego to glue relationships. Some comforting words or a gentle touch can be very reassuring.

Building Contacts versus Building Relationships

Many business schools today teach networking by suggesting that the graduates should join a chamber of commerce, Rotary, Lions, etc., in order to build contacts. If you ask the graduates why they are building contacts, the answer is that it will be useful someday. However, when the usefulness goes, the friendship also goes. They have not been taught to differentiate between building contacts versus building relationships. They are also not taught that usefulness is a byproduct of relationships.

For example, I have an office in Singapore. One day, I came from dinner and somebody met me in the lobby and asked me, 'Mr. Khera, did you go for dinner?' And I said yes. He followed up with a second question: 'Did you meet some people tonight?' My answer was yes. Then the man said something that really angered me. 'I hope the people you met tonight would be useful to you.' I felt like giving him a piece of my mind. This person's criterion for meeting people was their usefulness, that is, what he could extract out of them. Such people are only takers. He did not understand that usefulness is a byproduct of relationships.

Supposing I have a friend of twenty years. Tonight if he has a problem, who is the person he will most naturally go to for help? Obviously, to the friend of twenty years; he is not going to make new friends tonight. Is it my duty to help at this time? The answer is yes. If I help him, am I doing a favor? The answer is no. And if I don't help him, am I behaving like a friend? The answer is no. Remember, helping a friend is the duty of a friend but never the purpose of friendship. However, if that is the purpose, then the moment the purpose finishes, the friendship also finishes. That means there was no real friendship to begin with; there was a hidden agenda from the beginning. Be careful of people who are too sweet and over-friendly. They have hidden agendas.

People with healthy relationships:

- Trust and respect each other
- Make time for each other
- Collaborate as a team
- Help each other in accomplishing a task
- Engage in healthy activities together
- Focus on mutual benefits
- Listen to each other
- Have a caring attitude
- Let a relationship become a support group to overcome crisis
- Avoid loneliness
- Have a fulfilling and a meaningful life

A couple that was married for fifty-five years was asked, 'What is the secret of your happy married life?' The lady replied, 'We don't hate each other on the same day.'

Build relationships. Learn to socialize without any agenda. I remember there was a time when people would drop into each other's homes just to socialize. Many times it would happen without prior calling or confirmation. It was a very simple and relaxing way to connect with each other. A friend or neighbor dropping in was not unusual. There was no agenda; just being together was the agenda. The social interaction was enriching. Today socializing has taken the form of expensive and elaborate arrangements of entertainment. People don't find the time for simple things.

When you socialize with like-minded people, it relaxes you and helps you take up life's challenges more effectively.

Building strong relationships is crucial to one's well-being.

Your interpersonal skills are a good indicator of your ability to handle stress. We are quick to blame others for bad relationships, not realizing that generally it is a two-way street. For a relationship to go awry, each person plays a role. For example, A may say something casually, without meaning to hurt, but B may be quick to take offense. That is the starting point of a battle that will escalate. Control over your emotions can help break this cycle or mitigate such misunderstandings. A relaxed person is more unlikely to take offense and will give the other person the benefit of the doubt.

Remember, human relationships are vital for our mental and emotional well-being.

ACTIVITY

1. Identify one major take-home from this chapter.

   _____

   _____

   _____

2. Identify a relationship in your life that you have neglected. How can you fix it?

   _____

   _____

   _____

52

Cultivate Patience

Patience is not something that you perform or possess. It is a way of life. It is a conscious act. There is a big difference between patience and laziness. Some people are outright lazy, but they pretend they are patient.

Learn to live with short-term pain for long-term gain. Today the world is moving very fast, and media encourages instant gratification. Even waiting at a traffic light and standing at check-in or check-out counters has become unbearable. There are people honking at the traffic light as if that will make the light change faster. We have become more demanding, expecting faster service, and when that does not happen, we feel frustrated, angry and stressed out.

A patient person should avoid the following behaviors:

- Being a yes-man
- Being tolerant of ill-treatment
- Being non-assertive
- Being a doormat
- Becoming passive and over-submissive
- Having no self-respect

A patient person has the ability to overcome challenges without getting frustrated. They are able to control their emotions and impulsiveness. Hence they avoid damage and take mature decisions.

- The biggest advantage in being patient is that it bypasses impulsive decisions and actions
- It shows respect for the other person's feelings
- It gives time to understand things before reacting
- Patience also teaches us the ability to stay calm

Patience demonstrates self-control and emotional maturity.

ACTIVITY

1. Identify one major take-home from this chapter.

    _____

    _____

    _____

2. Identify three areas of improvement in your life.

    _____

    _____

    _____

53

Have a Good Night's Sleep

Sleepless and restless nights can be both a cause and a consequence of stress. When we are not relaxed, we cannot sleep, and when we cannot sleep, we have a restless night. The next day our stress level is very high. We become irritable, productivity goes down and it becomes a cycle.

Sound sleep improves our physical, mental and emotional health. Lack of quality sleep over time raises the risk of diseases and disorders such as heart disease and stroke, obesity and dementia. Sleep is a biological need for the body. That is when the body rests and recharges. **Lack of sleep impairs our ability to make good judgments and take mature decisions.** Inadequate sleep leads to both physical and mental exhaustion.

Most people need a strong cup of tea or coffee to get started in the morning because when they wake up they are tired to begin with. They just drag themselves out of bed and somehow manage to reach the office. They get their second and third doses of caffeine at the office and keep pumping caffeine all day long. No wonder they are restless at night.

Some people sleep every night with relaxation, whereas others sleep out of exhaustion. Someone I know was having major relationship problems within the family, and he was having sleepless nights. To get out of that, he started an exercise program and started riding his bicycle 50 miles every night so that when he came home, he was totally tired and went off to sleep out of exhaustion. Those who sleep out of relaxation wake up fresh and energized, and those who sleep out of exhaustion wake up tired and fatigued.

Sleep Recipe

Every night before going to sleep I switch off all the lights and keep only my bedside lamp on and read a book. As far back as I can remember, every night I have read ten to fifteen pages of a good self-help book. Please note, positive and relaxing, not thrilling and chilling. It works well, and within a short time, I fall asleep.

Some people are unable to sleep because of medical reasons or sleep disorders, and they need to get medical assistance.

Sleep is the best meditation. It provides vitality.

ACTIVITY

1. Identify one major take-home from this chapter.

    _____

    _____

    _____

2. Identify three steps to get a relaxed night's sleep.

    _____

    _____

    _____

Sometimes, to speed up, you need to slow down.

54

Live in the Present but With a Vision for the Future

The wealthiest person in the world cannot erase the past nor prepone the future. It is well said that a fired bullet, a spoken word and lost time cannot be retrieved.

We need to enjoy our present moments, because these are the only ones we can live in. We need to enjoy the gifts we have: our health, family, friends and work. Face the responsibilities and duties at hand without regrets of the past and worry for the future.

Live your life without guilt and resentment. That can only happen when you live in the present.

Our mind is like a monkey. It is everywhere but not where it should be. We constantly struggle to be physically present at one place while we are mentally elsewhere. We need to learn from the past, plan for the future but live in the present moment.

Advantages of living in the present:

- Reduces stress
- Leads to better relationships
- Improves productivity
- Makes a person proactive
- Helps become solution-focused

We need to bring equilibrium between the past, the present and the future.

Don't fret about tomorrow and regret yesterday. Focusing on the present brings clarity and calmness, allowing us to handle challenges in a mature manner. Staying in the present takes practice.

If yesterday was lost in grief, why lose your today or tomorrow by keeping them in your memory?

This life does not have a rewind button. Every fruitful moment in the present creates the seed for a better tomorrow.

ACTIVITY

1. Identify one major take-home from this chapter.

   _____

   _____

   _____

2. All through the day, every hour, pause and evaluate
   if you are fully operating in the present.

   _____

   _____

   _____

Remember,
yesterday is history,
tomorrow is a
mystery and today is
a gift.
That is why we call it
present.

55

Emotional Stability

Emotional stability serves as the pillar of support for partners needing stability in challenging times. Emotional stability builds better relationships.

With the world changing at the pace that it is, the degradation of values has led to emotional instability.

Some people are ill-tempered and obnoxious. They will always remain carriers of stress.

Once a man was unwell. So his wife let him rest and sleep till late in the morning. Her intention was to let him rest; hence she did not wake him up till noon. He woke up with a nasty temper, totally resentful and mad at his wife, demanding to know why he was not woken up. It ruined the entire atmosphere in the house, and nobody came to ask if he would like to have breakfast. He spread the negativity everywhere. The reverse happened the next day. Since he was still unwell, his wife woke him up at 11 a.m., thinking he had had enough sleep, and it would be useful for him to wake up and have some breakfast and gain some strength. Again, he woke up with a nasty temper, shouting that even though he was unwell she didn't let him sleep.

This only shows that due to his obnoxious temperament he was hard to please. People like him are unpredictable, moody, whimsical and imbalanced and display erratic behavior. Such people are all sugar and honey to you today and out to get your throat tomorrow.

In this and other similar instances, we need to ask these questions:

- What is the problem?
- Where is the problem?
- Who is creating the problem?

The source of such problems is usually the negative attitude of the person involved. They are the originators and carriers of stress. Whatever they do and wherever they go, they carry their negative aura and spread negativity like a plague. These are toxic people.

Emotional stability helps people handle stress more effectively. Instead of becoming overwhelmed by difficult situations, emotionally stable individuals can manage their emotions, stay calm and find productive solutions.

ACTIVITY

1. Identify one major take-home from this chapter.

   _____

   _____

   _____

2. Identify three behaviors you will change in yourself to build emotional stability.

   _____

   _____

   _____

3. How do you define stability in your personal and professional life?

   _____

   _____

   _____

4. What steps will you take to bring stability in your life?

   _____

   _____

   _____

56

This Too Shall Pass

Approach every problem with this philosophy: this too shall pass; it is not the end of the world.

Remember, every situation in life is temporary. So when life is good, make sure you enjoy and live fully. Also when life is not so good, remember it will not last forever. Better days are coming.

Once a king called all the scholars in his court and asked them to give a philosophy to live by. Some came up with a five-book-long answer. Some came up with a twelve-book-long answer. The king said, 'No, no, that is too much for me to read.' Then they came up with one book. The king said, 'It is too much for me to read.' Then they further condensed it to five pages. The king said, 'It is too much for me to read.' Then they came up with one page. The king was still not satisfied. Then an elderly person came and wrote one line on a paper: 'This too shall pass.' He folded it and gave it to the king. The king opened the folds and said, 'That's it. This is the way of life.'

Good times or bad times, they all come and go. When we are facing adversity, this is a great philosophy to live by: **this too shall pass.**

This too shall pass means the human condition is temporary and that neither positive nor negative moments in life last forever.

ACTIVITY

1. Identify one major take-home from this chapter.

   _____

   _____

   _____

2. Next time you are under stress remember the philosophy of this too shall pass and it will help.

57

Deep Breathing and Meditation

If you are familiar with the Lamaze method of natural childbirth, then you may be familiar with the powerful breathing techniques that help relax a person. Such breathing techniques can relax both the body and the mind within seconds.

Meditation is defined as the mind being in a state of emptiness. There are many benefits of meditation.

- It produces beneficial changes in our body that lower blood pressure
- It gives you a sense of calm, peace and balance that can benefit your emotional well-being and your overall health

To some stress is a habit and to others relaxation is a habit. The greatest investment one can make is to devote approximately fifteen minutes a day to meditation.

Many times relieving physical tension also helps relieve mental tension. A pleasant thought, a positive message, a peaceful picture, all help to clear the mind. Deep breathing slowly will also help to clear the mind. Our mind by its very nature can only focus on one thing at a time. If we keep a positive thought in the mind, the body starts responding in a relaxed manner. The reverse is just as true – a negative thought immediately stresses our body.

Meditation can give you a sense of calmness and inner peace. Meditation enhances emotional well-being and overall health.

ACTIVITY

1. Identify one major take-home from this chapter.

    _____

    _____

    _____

2. How do you plan to use breathing exercises and
    meditation to handle stress?

    _____

    _____

    _____

58

Avoid Distractions

Concentrate and stay focused. *Would you like to be operated by a surgeon who has two mobiles in his hands? With one, he is talking to his stockbroker – 'Which one should I buy or which one should I sell?' And on the other, he is talking with his wife, asking, 'What's for dinner tonight?' At the same time he is operating on your kidney. Imagine the outcome. Isn't that the way we behave in our real life?*

An unfocused mind is like a monkey jumping from one tree to another. We try to do one thing but the mind goes elsewhere, and we are not able to focus on anything. This is called an undisciplined mind, and it is constantly distracted. An uncontrolled mind wanders into the past from the future, thinking what could, should, would have happened, distracting us from the important tasks at hand. These disorderly thoughts can be very negative and only compound the problem. **Lack of concentration results in poor judgments, bad decisions and low productivity.**

Multitasking does not mean doing many things at the same time. That is a recipe for disaster. Multitasking means having the ability to do multiple things but doing them only one at a time.

The key to success is to avoid distractions and focus on priorities.

Distraction increases our chances of making errors. Relaxed people can focus much better and improve their output and the quality and quantity of output.

Stop attracting distractions.

ACTIVITY

1. Identify one major take-home from this chapter.

    _____

    _____

    _____

2. How do you plan to form the habit of concentration?

    _____

    _____

    _____

3. What benefit do you see from it?

    _____

    _____

    _____

59

Don't Sweat the Small Stuff

Many years ago, I heard a talk by a famous cardiologist by the name of Dr. Elliott. He was a doctor's doctor, teaching cardiology. He was always in the fast lane, traveling from one city to another, from one limousine to the aircraft to another limousine. One morning, he landed in a town and went to the hospital where he was going to address other doctors. He felt a little pain in his chest. Being a cardiologist, he could understand that this could be a problem. So he went to the nurses' station and asked the nurse to check him. He found out he was having a heart attack. Needless to say, he could not address the doctors, and he was admitted to the hospital.

Dr. Elliott was in his forties when this happened. Later, he said that the heart attack was the best thing that ever happened to him. He was doing the exact opposite of everything he was teaching. He was telling others to slow down, while he was himself in the fast lane. He said he had a wonderful wife but did not have any time to spend with her. He had two lovely daughters whom he never saw because they were sleeping every time he left home and came back. He never spent time with them or saw them grow up. He never took the time to smell the roses outside his window. He concluded that he had learned two lessons from his heart attack:

- *Don't sweat the small stuff.*
- *It's all small stuff.*

Can we say from the example of Dr. Elliott that sometimes we need to suffer pain before we learn our lesson?

I respect Dr. Elliott's message and the spirit behind it. However, it does not mean the person should have an indifferent or a casual attitude. Casual attitude always leads to casualty. Our responsibilities to ourselves, our family and society cannot and should not be taken casually.

Put your heart into what is important but don't let it give you a heart attack.

ACTIVITY

1. Identify one major take-home from this chapter.

   _____

   _____

   _____

2. Identify three areas of your life where you can practice 'don't sweat the small stuff'.

   _____

   _____

   _____

Notes

1. https://www.stress.org/workplace-stress/#:~:text=An%20estimated%201%20million%20workers,employees%20thinking%20about%20their%20stressors.
2. Ibid.
3. Ibid.
4. https://www.forbes.com/sites/susanadams/2013/04/09/stressed-out-at-work-its-getting-worse-study-shows/#:~:text=Some%2083%25%20of%20American%20workers,to%20the%20survey%3A%20low%20pay.
5. Khera, *You Can Win*, 206.
6. https://www.forbes.com/health/mind/mental-health-statistics/; https://www.nimh.nih.gov/health/statistics/mental-illness; https://www.ehstoday.com/health/article/21917550/burnt-out-stress-on-the-job- infographic
7. https://hms.harvard.edu/news/half-worlds-population-will-experience-mental-health-disorder
8. https://www.who.int/health-topics/mental-health#tab=tab_2
9. https://news.gallup.com/poll/505745/depression-rates-reach-new-high
10. https://www.stress.org/workplace-stress#:~:text=Depression%20and%20anxiety%20cost%20the,%2C%20diminished%20productivity%2C%20and%20accidents
11. https://www.cdc.gov/niosh/docs/99-101/default.html#:~:text=Nearly%20half%20of%20large,management%20training%20their%20workforces
12. https://www.scientificamerican.com/article/why-diets-don-t-work-and-what-to-do#:~:text=At%20any%20

given%20time%2C%20at,more%20weight%20after%20t
hey%20quit.

13. https://www.cnbc.com/2023/02/10/85-year-harvard-
study-found-the-secret-to-a-long-happy-and-successful-
life.html

14. https://www.huffpost.com/entry/time-management_
b_3176011

15. Khera, *You Can Win*, 222.

16. https://www2.deloitte.com/us/en/pages/about-deloitte/
articles/burnout-survey.html

17. https://www.who.int/news/item/28-05-2019-burn-out-
an-occupational-phenomenon-international-classification-
of-diseases

Enquire about our public and in house programs, Business Consulting and Motivational Gift items

Please contact me/send me information on

- Public Programs
  - Hi-Impact Leadership – Blueprint for success
  - Mastering Selling Skills & Develop Customer Service Excellence
  - Public speaking & Presentation skills
- Keynote Presentations
- In House Programs
- Business Consulting
- Audio, Video CDs/DVDs
- Books
- Motivational Gifts and Collector items

Name ....

Title ....

Company ....

Address ....

City .... State .... Pin Code ....

Telephone (O) .... Mobile ....

Email: ....

Qualified Learning Systems

C - 6/4, Vasant Vihar, New Delhi – 110057, INDIA
Phone: +91-11-47200200
E-mail: shivkhera@shivkhera.com
Visit us at **www.shivkhera.com**

Call us for special benefits for Bulk/Corporate Purchase